A PERIGEE BOOK
Published by the Penguin Group
Penguin Group (USA) LLC
375 Hudson Street, New York, New York 10014

USA • Canada • UK • Ireland • Australia • New Zealand • India • South Africa • China

penguin.com

A Penguin Random House Company

Perigee commemorative trade paperback edition ISBN: 978-0-399-17428-5

The Library of Congress has cataloged the first Perigee hardcover edition as follows:

Flaherty, Tina Santi.
What Jackie taught us : lessons from the remarkable life of Jacqueline Kennedy Onassis /
The Santi Flaherty—1st Perigee ed.
p. cm.
ISBN 0-399-52988-8
1. Onassis, Jacqueline Kennedy, 1929–1994. 2. Celebrities—United States—Biography.
3. Presidents' spouses—United States—Biography. I. Title.
CT275.O552F58 2004
973.922'092—dcc   2003064783

PUBLISHING HISTORY
First Perigee hardcover edition / April 2004
Perigee trade paperback edition / April 2005
Perigee commemorative hardcover edition / May 2014
Perigee commemorative trade paperback edition / May 2015

PRINTED IN THE UNITED STATES OF AMERICA

10 9 8 7 6 5 4 3 2 1

Most Perigee books are available at special quantity discounts for bulk purchases for sales
promotions, premiums, fund-raising, or educational use. Special books, or book excerpts, can
also be created to fit specific needs. For details, write: Special.Markets@us.penguingroup.com.

What Jackie Taught Us

What Jackie Taught Us

LESSONS FROM
THE REMARKABLE
LIFE OF
JACQUELINE
KENNEDY ONASSIS

Commemorative Edition

Tina Santi Flaherty

A PERIGEE BOOK

*To my dear brother Robert Alexander Santi, whose life—
like Jacqueline Kennedy Onassis's—inspires us to be
the best that we can be. On July 11, 2003, more than one
thousand people crowded into a small church in Memphis, Tennessee, to say their final farewell to a man who
would have been amazed that so many people cared.
His life, as did Jackie's, ended far too early, and, like her,
he tried in his own way to make the world a better place.*

I think they both succeeded.

Contents

PROLOGUE

SOME MAY BELIEVE that there is such a thing as "the Kennedy Curse." Violent deaths, personal destruction, and broken dreams have haunted the fabled family over the decades and have contributed to this belief. Whether this scourge actually exists is open to interpretation. There is no doubt, however, that Jacqueline Kennedy Onassis could rightfully be called "the Kennedy Blessing." Indeed, America was blessed in a way it had never been before her tenure as First Lady. In sharing with us her love and protection of all things beautiful, she changed the way America was perceived at home and abroad. For more than five decades, Jackie—as we still fondly call her—captured our imaginations as no other woman has or probably ever will again in our time. Her death in 1994 seemed premature, and it still doesn't seem fair that she's gone. Twenty years later, her radiant smile and elegant spirit continue to live on and will forever be a part of American history.

Jackie had everything people admired and wanted for themselves—beauty, intelligence, adorable children, a life full of excitement and glamour, and, yes, a handsome husband, John Fitzgerald Kennedy. We cannot think of Jackie without remembering Jack. Together they symbolized a poignant time in our nation's history, when its innocence and optimism promised that anything was possible. They gave us hope and made us feel that each of us would be the best we could be.

The extraordinary life of Jacqueline Kennedy Onassis was full of magic, both black and white. The most terrible tragedy that could ever be imagined happened to her. Her husband, the most powerful man in the free world, was murdered before her very eyes. She handled his death with a majesty that we will never forget. Our hearts ached as we tearfully reached out to her, young Caroline, and the little boy we called John-John. We loved Jackie when Jack was alive and continued to love her after he was gone. Admittedly, many of her admirers were temporarily thrown off base by her subsequent marriage to Greek shipping tycoon Aristotle Onassis. After Onassis died, we resumed our unflagging adoration when she emerged as America's most famous working woman. Jacqueline Kennedy Onassis was by no means a perfect person, but in our minds and memories, she was as close to perfection as few people ever will be.

Although I didn't know Jackie personally, I happened to live in the same building in New York City. In 1989, my former husband and I purchased an apartment at 1040 Fifth Avenue, the building to which Jacqueline Kennedy Onassis moved with her two children in 1964, after she left Washington, DC. With its magnificent views of Central Park and its large gracious apartments, 1040 Fifth was designed by the architectural genius Rosario Candela, who created some of New York City's most prestigious buildings, including the grand art deco duplex at 740 Park Avenue where Jackie lived as a child. Located on the Upper East Side of Manhattan, near the world-famous Metropolitan Museum of Art, 1040 Fifth Avenue is still special because to most people it's where Jacqueline Kennedy Onassis lived for the final thirty years of her life and it was there that she died in 1994 at the age of sixty-four.

As a neighbor, I observed Jackie from a faraway closeness— never wanting to encroach on her privacy. Once, her son, John, who was thirty-two years old at the time, approached me in the lobby as I was returning home from a chilly winter walk in Central Park with Liam, my yellow Labrador. "What's it like to have a dog in a New York City apartment?" he asked, with an earnest, friendly smile on his handsome face. "It's just fine," I answered. "Dogs just want to be wherever you are." It was an endearing encounter. I assumed he asked the question because he was thinking of getting a dog, which he subsequently did—an enormous German shepherd named Sam, which he rescued from the pound.

Jackie's Legacy

As a woman who filled many roles in her life, Jackie's enduring legacy lies in the choices she made. She handled happiness and heartache, incredible fame and wealth, and public demands and private needs with a remarkable discipline derived from a tremendous well of self-knowledge and acceptance. Indeed, Jackie taught the world, both women and men alike, many valuable lessons for which we may be forever grateful.

This book explores the unique path that Jacqueline Kennedy Onassis took, which led to her overwhelming success, and examines those personal characteristics and traits that made it possible. Her life shows us that success is determined less by an inborn capacity than by focus, strategy, and passion. More important for us, Jackie laid out a road map for achievement.

While we need not aspire to the same heights she reached to learn from her extraordinary accomplishments, we can all enlarge and enrich our own personal universe by following her example in our own way.

Veiling Truth in Mystery: An Introduction

Liz Smith is a celebrated columnist and the bestselling author of the memoir *Natural Blonde*.

*I*N MY SIXTY-ODD-YEAR career of writing about celebrities and the prominent, I've realized I've had the chance to observe the lives of five of the most famous and vital women of the twentieth and twenty-first centuries:

Marilyn Monroe, more famous now than when she died dramatically in 1962. Elizabeth Taylor, movie star of stars, and my friend, who left us in 2011. The still provocative pop queen deluxe Madonna, constantly pronounced "finished," who made more money last year than her younger competitors. Princess Diana, declared the VIP most people would like to bring back to life after her tragic early death in 1997. And Jacqueline Bouvier Kennedy Onassis—the most mysterious and inexplicable of them all—gone of illness in 1994.

Virgil wrote about "veiling truth in mystery," and Jackie's legacy has been just that.

This commemorative edition of *What Jackie Taught Us*, published on the twentieth anniversary of Jackie's death, includes not only the insights from her life about how to live with poise, grace, and zest as Tina Flaherty articulated them but also the memories of her by a number of astute observers. But this book won't pretend to solve the variousness, the depth of unusual ideas, theories, and contradictions about Jackie.

For she alone of the five maintained an almost impenetrable air of reticence and spiritual-psychic secrets. One way or another, the other four were flamboyant exhibitionists. But Jackie gave away only what she wanted people to know and think, and she left us always wanting more.

The world press almost went crazy because—though millions read the rumors that she was indifferent to infidelities, or promiscuous herself, and all the rest of her contradictions during her thousand days as First Lady—she gave up almost nothing. Her voice, downy and pillow soft, her televised tour of the White House with Charles Collingwood, her heroic behavior at the Dallas assassination, a final move to New York City to escape the public, the downhill phase of her marriage to Aristotle Onassis, and her private life as a book editor raising two first-rate children—Jackie never gave anything away.

If she did say something in a rare unintended interview—as with Teddy White and to William Manchester after JFK's death—she soon relented and denied it. Or sued to keep it quiet. Even the indefatigable Barbara Walters, who won the elusive Katharine Hepburn, never got to ask Jackie what kind of a tree she'd like to have been.

Jackie didn't exactly despise her fame; she just didn't want to cooperate with it unless on her own terms. She evidently knew who she was, and she didn't have to massage her ego or maintain and extend curiosity about herself. So she never did.

Thus the plethora of rumors continued: she spent a fortune on lingerie; she accepted a million to stay married to Jack; she had an affair with her brother-in-law; she told the famous writer Philip Roth when he dared kiss her cheek, "Oh, what did you have to do that for?" and dismissed him; she said or didn't say to the Metropolitan Museum, "I don't give a shit about the Temple of Dendur."

She did protect her privacy to a large extent. Even the persistent Ron Gallela, deemed "the Godfather of U.S. paparazzi culture" by *Time* magazine, finally—and legally—had to keep his distance. (He says now she should have paid him for the iconic hair-blowing shot of her walking away looking mysterious!)

I, for one, kept my distance and declared her son and daughter off limits. I was told she read my columns with relish, and Lyndon Johnson aide Horace Busby told me she adored gossip and mostly looked on life as a kind of French film farce. She told our mutual pal Joe Armstrong that "the

Kennedys will never forgive Liz Smith for writing about Jack and Judith Campbell Exner." But she seemed not to include herself in their number.

In time, I was introduced to her at book parties after she became an editor. I would see her often at get-togethers, social and charitable. I always stayed away from her at these gatherings, but I got the impression that she would seek me out—ask in a friendly complimentary manner who did my hair or talk about our mutual avidity for books on Austrian and middle European history or her charitable interests, like saving Grand Central Terminal. She even sent me nice handwritten notes when I mentioned her authors and books.

On the night I was given the Municipal Art Society Medal of Honor, I wondered if, as she hung the award around my neck, she might want to wring my neck instead. But she simply said, "Congratulations, Liz!" and moved on. She was the eternal sphinx.

Jackie is the star about whom I feel it has become almost pointless even to speculate. Usually humorous unless crossed, I am told she could turn as cold as ice and people were hard-pressed to know what they had done. According to her Secret Service man, Clint Hill, she was an angel, and he couldn't do enough to please her. According to the recent biography *These Few Precious Days: The Final Year of Jack with Jackie* by Chris Andersen, she was miserable at Jack's infidelities but adjusted in the White House until tragedy struck. In *Nemesis*, Peter

Evans's book about Onassis, he reports that Jackie went to his funeral with a curious half-smile on her face, causing his daughter, Christina, to leap out of the car she was sharing with her father's enigmatic widow. Jackie didn't explain.

She never spoke for herself. She didn't give interviews. The press and public had to do all the work. That is something like mining for gold—forever—without hitting pay dirt. But still, she seems rich in spirit and personality beyond our wildest dreams. It is only in dreams that she really exists and in our imaginations. She didn't allow much of anything more.

At the end, her best personal revelation about her illness was only this: "Why did I bother to do all those push-ups and exercise before non-Hodgkin's lymphoma!" She died as she had lived, privately, with family, friends, and her long-time companion, Maurice Tempelsman, by her side. Of her death, her son, John, said that she died "in her own way, on her own terms, and we all feel lucky for that."

The most attractive, exasperating, intelligent, frustrating historical icon ever. She was the First Lady to end all First Ladies for never giving herself away.

—Liz Smith

What Jackie Taught Us

Jackie Revisited

———

It is twice as hard to crush a half-truth as a whole lie.

—UNKNOWN

*M*ANY DIFFERENT PERCEPTIONS exist about the life of Jacqueline Kennedy Onassis. One is that Jackie was merely a beautiful woman whose life was consumed with shopping and traveling to glamorous places. Nothing could be further from the truth.

As with many attractive women whose intelligence and accomplishments are often hidden behind their glamour and style, Jackie's keen intellect was often obscured by her jetsetting image and her big, dark sunglasses. In 1962, a *New York Times* article grudgingly acknowledged Jackie's intelligence with this comment: "It is now all right for a woman to be a bit brainy or cultured as long as she tempers her intelligence with a 't'rific' girlish rhetoric."

As a young woman, Jackie learned to conceal her intellect,

perhaps believing her mother's advice that men don't like brainy women. When she met her husband-to-be, Jack Kennedy, she found that wasn't necessarily true.

What Jackie achieved in her thousand days in the White House was monumental in scope. Through her style, her grace, and her impassioned support of the arts as well as her key role in historic preservation, she helped change the way America was perceived by the rest of the world.

Although Jackie was destined to be a major player on the world stage, she began her life in a very ordinary setting, a small hospital on the eastern shore of Long Island.

Early Years

From the beginning, it appeared that Jackie somehow wanted to do things her way, even choosing the date of her birth. Due to arrive in mid-June, she was born six weeks later, on July 28, 1929, at the local hospital in the fashionable resort village of Southampton, about two hours from New York City. She was the first child of Janet Norton Lee and John "Jack" Vernou Bouvier III. Three months after her birth, the stock market crash of October 1929 occurred, turning the world upside down.

While only marginally affected by the Depression, Jackie's family soon suffered significant financial setbacks due to Jack Bouvier's careless investments and indiscriminate spending habits, creating a major change in their lifestyle. Jackie and her sister, Lee, born four years later, were left with a lifelong feeling of insecurity and a deep fear of poverty despite their relatively comfortable existence.

Although Jackie was born into a privileged lifestyle, the Bouviers were not descended from French nobility, as her grandfather stubbornly claimed. Instead, their ancestors, who originated in southern France, had been tailors, farmers, and even domestic servants. The name Bouvier, while suggesting aristocratic lineage, actually means "cowherd." Michel Bouvier, the family's first immigrant to America, left France in 1815 after serving in Napoleon's defeated army and settled in Philadelphia. Starting as a handyman, he later became a cabinetmaker and eventually a successful land speculator. His children and grandchildren prospered over the years, marrying into some of society's leading families, including the Ewings, Sergeants, and Drexels.

Contrary to popular opinion, Jackie was more Irish than French, an important point to note, given the later emphasis on her French ancestry. Her mother, Janet Lee, was 100 percent Irish. The Lee family had arrived in America in 1852 from County Cork, Ireland, at the time of the potato famine. Janet's maternal grandmother, Margaret Merritt, who cooked and cleaned for the Lee family, spoke with a thick Irish brogue, much to her granddaughter's embarrassment.

Although Jackie's father, John Vernou Bouvier III, had a surname that was totally Gallic, he was only one-quarter French, the rest being a mixture of Scottish and English. His daughter, Jackie, consequently, was only one-eighth French. His beloved mother, Maude Sergeant Bouvier, Jackie's grandmother, would tease her adored son whenever he was naughty about the unwholesome French blood he had inherited from his father. Jackie's cousin, John H. Davis, in his book, *The Bouviers: Portrait of an American Family,* describes an incident when Jack's father found him in the barn, pricking his finger and squeezing out drops of blood. "When asked what he was doing, he replied that he was trying to squeeze all the naughty French blood out of himself," writes Davis.

Mother Maude's influence was no match, however, for that of her husband, John Vernou Bouvier Jr. The Major, as he preferred to be called, told his children and grandchildren that they were descended from the kings and queens of France, belonging to the noble house of Fontaine. He went so far as to have a book, *Our Forbears*, printed to reinforce his claims. Jackie, as a young girl, might easily have bought into the myth that her French ancestors were of royal blood, although historians have disproved this lineage.

Whether Jackie acknowledged these genealogical truths or not doesn't really matter. Throughout her life she was an avid fan of history, realizing that the past offers lessons that can be applied to the present.

Even as a child, Jackie had a clear view of herself and a unique vision of life's possibilities. Given the choice, she preferred the company of horses and dogs to people. Her love of literature also surfaced early on. Instead of playing with dolls, she turned to books and counted Byron, Robin Hood, and Scarlett O'Hara among her heroes. One of her teachers was amazed to learn that six-year-old Jackie even enjoyed reading Chekhov's short stories.

School Days

Jackie attended the best private schools, starting at age six at the Chapin School for Girls. Her fellow classmates remember her as one of the brightest in their group. As recounted in Mary Van Rensselaer Thayer's book, *Jacqueline Bouvier Kennedy*, one of her teachers there recalled that she was "the prettiest little girl, very clever, very artistic and full of the devil." Unfortunately, none of these gifts helped ease her pain during the estrangement of her exacting mother and her hard-drinking, fast-spending, womanizing father.

Jackie's true joy was horses and riding, through which she revealed an intensely competitive nature and a total distaste for defeat. Already a budding championship rider who had first sat on a horse at the age of two, the stables became a welcome retreat for her. She was encouraged by her mother, Janet, an accomplished rider who competed in horse shows throughout the Northeastern states. Having inherited Janet's physical courage and love of competition, it was apparent that Jackie would be an excellent horsewoman. By age five, she had begun to compete and win blue ribbons on the riding circuit. In 1940, eleven-year-old Jackie won every event she entered in the under-twenty division, including two categories in the National Horse Show at Madison Square Garden.

That same year her parents finally divorced. Her mother's subsequent marriage in 1942 to a wealthy stockbroker, Hugh D. Auchincloss Jr., hurt Jackie deeply, as she adored her father, who felt the same way about her. Soon after the divorce, relatives noticed that Jackie began to withdraw into her own private world.

Later, Jackie attended Miss Porter's School in Farmington, Connecticut, where she studied art history, literature, and drawing and earned As in French and Spanish. She attracted as much attention for her intelligence as for her beauty. When she graduated from Miss Porter's, the yearbook recorded her stated ambition in life "not to be a housewife."

Debutante of the Year

Jackie was accepted by Vassar College in 1947 after scoring in the highest possible percentile on her College Board exams. Just before the fall term began, Igor Cassini, the influential and widely read New York society columnist, named her "Debutante of the Year." He glowingly described her as a "regal brunette who has classic features and the daintiness of Dresden porcelain." He also enthused about her poise and intelligence. In an era when society still counted, this accolade put Jackie near the level of a Hollywood star. She became an overnight celebrity, enjoying a steady swirl of society balls and grand parties.

After the heady atmosphere of the "season," she found life at Vassar, located in rural Poughkeepsie, New York, to be boring— even reportedly referring to it as "that damned Vassar." Nonetheless, Jackie was an excellent student, earning A+ in both a Shakespearean course and the history of religion. Much to her family's chagrin, Jackie decided not to attend Vassar for her junior year and applied to a program at Smith College for a year of study at the Sorbonne in France.

A Year in France

Jackie was accepted by Smith College's foreign study program and went to France in August 1949 for her junior year. Although somewhat proficient in French, Jackie did not have full command of its finer points. She and a few of the other participants were first sent to an intensive six-week language course at the University of Grenoble, about three hundred miles from Paris. In October, she arrived in the City of Light and began courses at the Sorbonne, all taught in French with a concentration on French history and art.

Years later, in the White House, Jackie would draw upon her time in Europe, re-creating the legendary, sophisticated parties she had attended in Paris that had magically mixed politicians, artists, movie stars, and society notables.

Return to the States

With her horizons broadened by her European experience, Jackie was determined not to return to Vassar, even though her father begged her to remain near his New York City residence. Instead, in 1950, she decided to enroll at George Washington University in Washington, DC, near her mother and stepfather's luxurious Virginia estate, Merrywood. Again, her independent thinking won out against the wishes of others.

While Jackie was completing work for her degree, she entered *Vogue* magazine's annual Prix de Paris competition, a writing contest with a top prize of working for a year as a junior editor—six months in New York and six months in the Paris office. She won the competition over 1,279 other contestants.

Supposedly, Jackie's first day of work at the *Vogue* office in New York was momentous. By midmorning, she had visited the personnel office and quit, saying that her mother felt strongly about keeping her at home. However, it is more likely, as one of her friends reported, that the decision was completely Jackie's. Once she had a close-up look at the overwhelmingly female environment of *Vogue*, it simply confirmed an early suspicion that the fashion world was not the best place for her—especially if she wanted to find a suitable man to marry.

First Job

Jackie, who was primarily dependent on her father's financial support, was always strapped for cash. After graduation from college in 1951, she badly needed a job to supplement her meager monthly allowance from him. Although Jackie's wealthy stepfather, Hugh D. Auchincloss Jr., paid for few of her day-to-day expenses, he was generous with his connections. Through him, she was able to secure an interview at the *Washington Times-Herald*, a lively, impertinent newspaper that was outselling both the *Washington Post* and *Evening Star* at the time. It also had the reputation of readily hiring attractive girls with modest expertise. At her interview with the city editor, Jackie was told that she could have the job of Inquiring Photographer if she managed to learn how to use a Speed Graphic camera by the following day. After an intense tutorial with the staff photographer, she got the job, beginning in January 1952 at $25 a week. Ironically, Kathleen Kennedy, Jack's sister, had once held the same job, as had Jack's former girlfriend, the voluptuous Inga Arvad, affectionately known as "Inga Binga" to Jack.

At about the same time, Jackie became engaged to John Husted, a family friend. Socially prominent, he had an impeccable WASP background and a promising career on Wall

Street. Their engagement was announced in January 1952. Almost immediately, however, Jackie had serious reservations. In truth, she did not want the life of an ordinary New York matron and, given her large ambition, was also not eager to be the wife of a traditional Wall Street businessman.

Although being the newspaper's Inquiring Photographer was not an intellectually demanding job, it required considerable creativity on Jackie's part, as her assignment was to ask people on the street or in their offices about a topic of the day and photograph them. In typical Jackie fashion, she took great care to prepare interesting, often personal questions to provoke equally interesting answers. She took her job seriously and wanted her column to reflect favorably on her. Once she posed the question, "Do you think a wife should let her husband think he's smarter than she is?" And "Chaucer said that what most women desire is power over men. What do you think women desire most?" She asked two other questions that were ominously prescient:

"Which first lady would you most like to have been?"

"What prominent person's death affected you most?"

Jackie and Jack

The job suited Jackie well, and it provided access to new and influential people. Using her newspaper column as a cover, she called tall, good-looking Jack Kennedy, then a senator, whom she had met at a dinner party in 1951. Since that first meeting, she had heard many stories about Jack Kennedy at the *Times-Herald*, including his war heroics and the fact that women found him irresistible.

Jackie's interview with the charismatic senator brought her to his attention again. Many people in Kennedy's office felt Jackie's column played a prominent part in rekindling their relationship. Within a short time she broke her engagement to John Husted, and the Bouvier/Kennedy romance took on a more serious note. According to Jack's prep school friend, Lem Billings, Jackie was more intelligent, literary, and substantial than most of the other young women Jack dated. She also had a certain classiness that Jack found very attractive.

As for Jack himself, he was any woman's dream come true. A popular three-term congressman and then a senator, he was intelligent, witty, and extremely wealthy. His father, Joseph P. Kennedy, former ambassador to the Court of St. James in London, was the twelfth richest man in America, having a net worth that *Fortune* magazine estimated at $400 million—the equivalent of several billion dollars in today's money. They had homes in Boston, New York, Palm Beach, and Cape Cod. What more could a woman want?

Jackie and Jack began seeing each other more often, and in January 1953, she was Jack's date at the inaugural ball of President Dwight D. Eisenhower. So taken was she that Jackie began sending Jack nutritious gourmet meals to his office to express her concern over his poor eating habits, along with buying him special books and doing everything she could to get his attention. Still, Jack showed no signs of proposing, much to Jackie's disappointment. But now it was Jackie's turn to play hard to get. Surprising Jack, she told him that she was taking an unexpected trip to London to cover the coronation of Queen Elizabeth II.

Leaving for England on May 22, 1953, the trip provided an excellent opportunity for Jackie to consider if she wanted to marry Jack after all. Cautioned by several trusted male friends about Jack's womanizing, she hoped that, once married, he would cease this behavior. Additionally, she knew that her life with him would always be interesting and that he also had the necessary financial resources to overcome her primal fear of poverty. As her former beau Demi Gates said, "she was absolutely obsessed with poverty." Another male friend said, "She had an insecurity about money, a fear of going back to being poor." Her mother, who was forced to work in a New York City department store after her divorce to help support herself and her two daughters before her marriage to Hugh D. Auchincloss Jr., continuously reinforced this concern. Janet Auchincloss had experienced life at both ends of the scale, with and without money. She was adamant that her daughters marry into "real" money.

Besides possessing wealth, Jackie wanted a husband who stimulated her mentally. Jack was a great conversationalist with an intellectual curiosity that appealed to Jackie. They shared a common love of books that they would enjoy throughout their lives. His reputation as a playboy did not concern Jackie, perhaps because she idolized her father, who had the same propensity. Jack had already decided that Jackie, with her "cool reserve, humor, and intelligence," would be the least likely woman to bore him. Their shared Catholic religion was important, too. In early June, when Jackie returned from London, Jack met her plane. Their engagement was announced on June 24, 1953.

Marriage to Jack

On September 12, 1953, Jackie Bouvier and Jack Kennedy were married at St. Mary's Church in Newport, Rhode Island. The wedding was stage-managed by Joe Kennedy, who saw it as an opportunity to further his son's political career. He was happy to pay for the event after convincing Jackie's mother, Janet, to disregard her daughter's wish for a small, simple wedding. Joe had crammed nine hundred guests into a church meant to hold only seven hundred and invited fourteen hundred to the reception—as well as dozens of photographers, reporters, and columnists.

Jackie wasn't even able to wear the kind of wedding gown she preferred. Favoring something simple with straight lines that would complement her tall, trim figure, she wore, instead, a traditional dress with a huge bouffant skirt because Jack's family wanted something more ornate. Later, she told a friend that she thought it made her look "like a lampshade." It was one of the rare occasions when the dress wore Jackie, not the other way around.

It was not a totally happy day for Jackie because her beloved father was reportedly too hungover to walk her down the aisle. There is some speculation that Janet had deliberately caused this. Rumor has it that she sent her son-in-law, Michael Canfield, who was married to her daughter Lee, to visit and drink with Jack Bouvier at his hotel the night before the wedding. Whether Janet asked Canfield to deliberately get him drunk is not definitively known. However, it was common knowledge that Jack Bouvier had a serious drinking problem and Janet did not want to take any chances, as she knew the wedding of her daughter to the handsome, young senator would be reported in great detail by the nation's press.

According to Jackie's sister, Lee, "My mother had written him [Jack Bouvier] telling him she hoped he realized that he was far from welcome and that he might change his mind and decide not to come, and she felt that this would be a far more appropriate thing for him to do." As was her penchant, Jackie concealed the hurt the episode caused her, instead displaying the courage and self-discipline for which she would later become famous.

After Jackie married John Fitzgerald Kennedy, the couple searched for a "little Georgetown house," which they ultimately found, and there they began their political life together in Washington, DC. Jackie did not take easily to political life and much preferred the world of arts and letters. That proclivity served Jack well as he began work on his book *Profiles in Courage.* According to the journalist and author Mary Van Rensselaer Thayer, "When Jack began sprouting ideas for the book, Jackie seized on it as a way of keeping him distracted from his back pain, and scribbled the notions down. It was she who successfully connected with Harper and Brothers publishers, who contracted to do the book, which went on to win the Pulitzer Prize."

Thayer, a friend of Jackie's and her mother, Janet, said that, "*Profiles in Courage* couldn't have happened without Jacqueline. She encouraged her husband, read to him, carried out independent research, and on lined yellow copy paper, wrote down parts of the book." Jackie was well-known for her meticulous organizational skills and kept a yellow lined notepad by her bed with lists of what she intended her staff to carry out. According to her White House secretary, Mary Barelli Gallagher, she "dogged people with her morning memos." Arthur M. Schlesinger Jr. once likened them to Churchill's "Action This Day" memos during World War II.

Jackie embarked on her journey that would take her from being a senator's bride to the world stage as the wife of the thirty-fifth President of the United States. Yet the greatest joys of her life would come from motherhood, with the birth of Caroline in 1957, followed by John Jr. in 1960.

Sadly, Jackie's marriage to Jack Kennedy ended ten years later with his assassination in 1963. Later, she would marry one of the world's richest men, Greek shipping tycoon Aristotle

Onassis. Their turbulent relationship ended with his death in 1975. Never to marry again, Jackie found fulfillment and happiness with Maurice Tempelsman, her long-time companion.

Public Works

Planning for the John F. Kennedy Presidential Library and Museum began immediately after the assassination of President Kennedy in 1963. From the beginning, Jackie was heavily involved in the development of the library, which opened its doors in 1979 in Columbia Point at Boston's waterfront. Jackie had a say in every element of the library, from fund raising to organizing exhibits and choosing the location and design of the building. It was her decision to use I. M. Pei as the architect, although he was relatively unknown and inexperienced at the time. She selected him over other better-known architects because she admired his individuality and once commented that she saw in Pei great promise and potential that reminded her of her late husband.

In 1975, Jackie became involved with the Municipal Art Society, a nonprofit organization devoted to historic preservation in New York. Her participation, perseverance, and celebrity status are credited for saving Grand Central Terminal, one of New York's most important and beautiful buildings, from the wrecking ball. She was also instrumental in bringing the ancient Temple of Dendur from Egypt to the Metropolitan Museum of Art.

Career as an Editor

Jackie had a lifelong passion for reading, and it is not surprising that after her marriage to Aristotle Onassis ended, she chose to devote herself to work in the publishing industry. Beginning in 1975, Jackie enjoyed a successful career as a book editor. Among the hundred books she edited covering a wide range of topics, from fashion to history to photography to religion, were such bestsellers as *Moonwalk* by Michael Jackson, Carly Simon's children's books, several works by Bill Moyers, and a trilogy by the Nobel Prize–winning Egyptian writer Naguib Mahfouz. Books were vital to Jackie. She once told Joe Armstrong, a friend and editor himself, "These [books] are my other best friends." Upon her death in May 1994, John Kennedy Jr. announced that his mother passed on "surrounded by her friends and her family and her books and the people and things that she loved."

Jackie lived her life with poise, grace, and zest, regardless of any pain or disappointment. In her own words, which are quoted in Andrew Roberts's essay on self-awareness:

But I have had lots of happy moments, as well. Every moment one lives is different from the other. The good, the bad, the hardship, the joy, the tragedy, love, and happiness are all interwoven into one single indescribable whole that is called life. You cannot separate the good from the bad. And perhaps there is no need to do so, either.

Special Tribute by Senator Edward M. Kennedy

Funeral Mass, Church of St. Ignatius Loyola, New York City
May 23, 1994

*L*AST SUMMER, WHEN we were on the upper deck on the boat at the Vineyard, waiting for President and Mrs. Clinton to arrive, Jackie turned to me and said: "Teddy, you go down and greet the President."

"But," I said, "Maurice is already there."

And Jackie answered: "Teddy, you do it. Maurice isn't running for re-election."

She was always there, for all our family, in her special way.

She was a blessing to us and to the nation—and a lesson to the world on how to do things right, how to be a mother, how to appreciate history, how to be courageous.

No one else looked like her, spoke like her, wrote like her, or was so original in the way she did things. No one we knew ever had a better sense of self.

Eight months before she married Jack, they went together to President Eisenhower's inaugural ball. Jackie said later that that's where they decided they liked Inaugurations.

No one ever gave more meaning to the title of First Lady. The nation's capital city looks as it does because of her. She saved Lafayette Square and Pennsylvania Avenue.

Jackie brought the greatest artists to the White House, and brought the arts to the center of national attention. Today, in large part because of her inspiration and vision, the arts are an abiding part of national policy.

President Kennedy took such delight in her brilliance and her spirit. At a White House dinner, he once leaned over and told the wife of the French Ambassador, "Jackie speaks fluent French. But I only understand one out of every five words she says—and that word is de Gaulle."

And then, during those four endless days in 1963, she held us together as a family and a country. In large part because of her, we could grieve and then go on. She lifted us up, and in the doubt and darkness, she gave her fellow citizens back their pride as Americans. She was then thirty-four years old.

Afterward, as the eternal flame she lit flickered in the autumn of Arlington Cemetery, Jackie went on to do what she most wanted—to raise Caroline and John, and warm her family's life and that of all the Kennedys.

Robert Kennedy sustained her, and she helped make it

possible for Bobby to continue. She kept Jack's memory alive, as he carried Jack's mission on.

Her two children turned out to be extraordinary, honest, unspoiled, and with a character equal to hers. And she did it in the most trying of circumstances. They are her two miracles.

Her love for Caroline and John was deep and unqualified. She reveled in their accomplishments, she hurt with their sorrows, and she felt sheer joy and delight in spending time with them. At the mere mention of one of their names, Jackie's eyes would shine brighter and her smile would grow bigger.

She once said that if you "bungle raising your children nothing else much matters in life." She didn't bungle. Once again, she showed how to do the most important thing of all, and do it right.

When she went to work, Jackie became a respected professional in the world of publishing. And because of her, remarkable books came to life. She searched out new authors and ideas. She was interested in everything.

Her love of history became a devotion to historic preservation. You knew, when Jackie joined the cause to save a building in Manhattan, the bulldozers might as well turn around and go home.

She had a wonderful sense of humor—a way of focusing on someone with total attention—and a little girl delight in who they were and what they were saying. It was a gift of herself that she gave to others. And in spite of all her heartache and loss, she never faltered.

I often think of what she said about Jack in December after he died: "They made him a legend, when he would have preferred to be a man." Jackie would have preferred to be just herself, but the world insisted that she be a legend, too.

She never wanted public notice, in part I think, because it brought back painful memories of an unbearable sorrow, endured in the glare of a million lights.

In all the years since then, her genuineness and depth of character continued to shine through the privacy to reach people everywhere. Jackie was too young to be a widow in 1963, and too young to die now.

Her grandchildren were bringing new joy to her life, a joy that illuminated her face whenever you saw them together. Whether it was taking Rose and Tatiana for an ice cream cone, or taking a walk in Central Park with little Jack as she did last Sunday, she relished being Grand Jackie and showering her grandchildren with love.

At the end, she worried more about us than herself. She let her family and friends know she was thinking of them. How cherished were those wonderful notes in her distinctive hand on her powder blue stationery!

In truth, she did everything she could, and more, for each of us.

She made a rare and noble contribution to the American spirit. But for us, most of all she was a magnificent wife, mother, grandmother, sister, aunt, and friend.

She graced our history. And for those of us who knew and loved her, she graced our lives.

1

What Jackie Taught Us About
Self-Awareness

KNOWING WHO YOU ARE

"No one else looked like her, spoke like her, or was so original in the way she did things. No one we knew ever had a better sense of self."
——SENATOR TED KENNEDY, MAY 23, 1994

TED KENNEDY'S EULOGY at the funeral of his sister-in-law lovingly and succinctly summarized the essence of Jackie's image. Because she knew who she was and what she wanted, she was able to accomplish more than most.

It's been said a thousand times—if you don't know where you want to go, you'll never get there. To achieve what you want out of life, you have to know what you believe in. As deceptively easy as it may sound, success begins and ends with knowing who you are and what you stand for.

Like many successful people, Jackie possessed a very strong

sense of self and was determined to follow the path of her own choosing. Sometimes it meant thwarting her often indomitable mother or disappointing her beloved father. As First Lady, it frequently meant refusing to give in to the demands of a wide universe of people who wanted something from her—relatives, the Kennedy family, her staff, political advisers, the media, and, of course, the American people. As a child, Jackie was fortunate to recognize what made her happy or sad, what she liked and disliked, and how she wanted to live her life. "I hated dolls, loved horses and dogs, and had skinned knees and braces on my teeth for what must have seemed an interminable length of time to my family," she recalled years later in a writing competition she won in 1951 at age twenty-one for *Vogue* magazine's Annual Prix de Paris.

Undoubtedly, Jackie's ability to recognize her strengths and weaknesses also contributed to her enormous success. She showed remarkable candor in acknowledging her vulnerabilities in the same essay when she wrote, "One of my most annoying faults is getting very enthusiastic over something at the beginning and then tiring of it halfway through. I am trying to counteract this by not getting too enthusiastic over too many things at once." This quality of knowing where she would most likely succeed or fail stayed with her throughout her life and is one of the major reasons that she achieved as much as she did.

As Jackie always had an urge to resist the status quo, it's not surprising that in response to another portion of the *Vogue* competition she named writer Oscar Wilde, poet Charles Baudelaire, and Russian ballet impresario Sergei Diaghilev—three unconventional men who were notorious for smashing bourgeois credos—as her choice for "People I wish I had known."

Ironically, Jackie's turbulent childhood was probably a major factor in motivating her to develop this sense of self-awareness. Her instinct for survival propelled her to create her own safe world, relying on intuition to find her way rather than following the path her parents took, which was filled with anger, disappointment, and infidelity.

Jackie's father, who spent money recklessly, has been described as "a fan of strong drink, fast horses, and beautiful women." He was a gregarious alcoholic who could not stop pursuing women, but at the same time, a loving and adoring parent who complimented and encouraged Jackie at every step of the way—in contrast to her mother, who was sparing in her praise. Her mother, unhappy and disillusioned with Jackie's philandering father, sometimes took out her frustration on their two daughters. Janet was a harsh disciplinarian who demanded perfection from herself and her children.

As a child, Jackie developed an inner toughness in the face of the public humiliation created by her father's behavior and her parents' bitter relationship. The fact that all the lurid details of their eventual divorce were reported in the press, along with a photo of eleven-year-old Jackie, only served to deepen her sense of resolve to develop a life for herself on her own terms.

As a result, riding horses became much more than just an enjoyable childhood activity for Jackie. It was an outlet for both physical exercise and mental escape. Years later, her father reportedly told Jackie's future husband, John Kennedy, "If you ever have any trouble with Jackie, put her on a horse." Despite suffering a number of mishaps, including a broken collarbone, a slipped disc, and a fall that knocked her unconscious, Jackie's dedication to riding never wavered. Because it was an activity in which she excelled, riding gave Jackie a renewed sense of self. She also credited horseback riding for the impeccable posture and regal carriage that defined her style as dramatically as her wardrobe.

Jackie's dysfunctional childhood taught her that she needed privacy and protection from the world at large if she were ever to feel secure. She also learned that reading and indulging in her passion for the arts would always be a comfort to her. For her to feel truly safe, however, financial security was paramount. Jackie's childhood years of watching her father's fortune dwindle, her parents arguing bitterly over money, and finally divorcing undoubtedly had a lifelong effect on her. Indeed, the memory of being wealthy and losing most of it must have produced in Jackie a fear that created an obsessive concern about money. Her sister Lee's opinion was that money was insulation. "She'd seen enough downfall around her to want that insulation."

Even after her mother married Hugh D. Auchincloss Jr., a multimillionaire heir to the Standard Oil fortune, money continued to be an issue for Jackie. Surrounded by wealth that was unavailable to them, she and her sister lived in the enormous Auchincloss houses in Virginia and Newport, Rhode Island, but they were considered stepchildren, not Auchinclosses, and did not have trust funds set up for them by their stepfather, as did the other children. Already, there were three Auchincloss children from Hugh's first two wives, and before long, there would be two more with his new wife, Janet. Jackie, far from being an heiress, except for room and board provided by Hugh D. Auchincloss Jr., was forced to depend financially on her father and grandfather.

Whenever Jackie did visit her father, she would feel sorry for him, especially when he continued to blame her mother for the loss of his money. It probably wasn't difficult for a young girl to believe that if only her father had more money, her parents would have loved each other and they would have been a happy family.

To the casual observer of Jackie's spending habits, particularly as an adult, it may be hard to imagine that a person concerned with financial security could have spent money as prodigiously as she did. In light of Jackie's constant quest for perfection and her need to be the best, money and all it brought was integral to her sense of well-being.

It's not surprising then that both of Jackie's husbands, Jack Kennedy and Aristotle Onassis, were wealthy and powerful—attributes possibly entwined in Jackie's mind with the premise that with financial security comes love and happiness. When, at age twenty-three, she met Jack Kennedy, she had found a man who was far more attractive to her than John Husted, the Wall Street businessman who had been her fiancé for a few short months. Harvard-educated and extremely good-looking, Jack shared Jackie's love of history and literature. His sharp repartee and easy laugh appealed to her well-developed sense of humor and quick wit. More important, he was already a powerful U.S. senator with rapidly ascending prospects for the future, and his family was among the wealthiest in the country.

Finding in each other an emotional haven, both had suffered the pain of cold, distant mothers and blatantly unfaithful fathers, which undoubtedly affected their outlooks on love and marriage. Although Jackie, a tall, slim, dark-haired beauty, was nothing like the bosomy blondes with whom Jack usually spent time, he was captivated by her manner, both enticing and elusive, and her deep appreciation of literature and history. Her patrician air and connection to the WASP milieu was also extremely appealing.

Although Jackie was raised in an era when women were taught to camouflage their strengths lest they turn off men, she fully recognized her strong suits and always played to them. She realized early on that it was the best way to handle the Kennedy family, who liked to be associated with winners. Their father, Joseph Kennedy, instilled competition in the children at an early age. He frequently reminded them, "We don't want any losers around here." When she first began dating Jack, he invited her to play in a game of touch football at the Kennedy compound in Hyannisport, Cape Cod. She decided to give it a try and proceeded to break her ankle. Instead of improving her skills to impress Jack, she didn't play again, as she realized rough-and-tumble sports were not her cup of tea.

Often the Kennedy brothers and sisters would be engaged in fierce competition in swimming, sailing, softball, or golf, and Jackie would opt to read a good book or paint a picture—pastimes to which she was much better suited. When Jack asked her to join his crew for the annual Labor Day Hyannisport Yacht Club Regatta, she refused, telling him, "It's enough for me to enjoy a sport without having to win, place or show." This was not entirely true, as Jackie was a fierce competitor. It was probably difficult for her to admit to Jack that she didn't want to crew with him because she was not as good at it as he was. However, Jackie maintained her reputation as a sportswoman by indulging in activities in which she excelled—horseback riding, in particular, as well as waterskiing and swimming.

Armed with the confidence of knowing that he was the

right man for her, Jackie proceeded to campaign for the job of Jack's wife until she succeeded. With their marriage, a union was forged that history will never forget.

Not particularly interested in politics, it hardly seemed likely that Jackie would leave such a lasting legacy after serving as First Lady for only three short years. However, because Jackie knew her strengths, she was able to effectively deploy them to help her husband and the image of his presidency.

In undertaking the restoration of the White House, Jackie chose a project that she understood completely and one in which she knew she was destined to shine. As one of her biographers remarked, "It was a part of Jackie's genius and an important quality in her role in restoring the White House that she not only had an instinctive feel for what was right for the house, but also knew exactly where to go for advice and who to approach for help."

From her mother, Janet Auchincloss, Jackie inherited the knowledge of how a grand home should be furnished and run. Janet, now married to a wealthy stockbroker, managed and artfully decorated spectacular estates at Merrywood in Virginia and at Hammersmith Farms in Rhode Island. Jackie absorbed all this information as a young girl and learned to insist on the best.

Her mother had also taught her how to entertain with style and flair. Consequently, Jackie had no fear when it came to organizing magnificent state dinners in the White House, honoring kings, queens, prime ministers, and other world leaders.

Because Jackie was true to her inner beliefs, she was able to accomplish her goals in the brief time she served as First Lady. She actively pursued what made her happy and often avoided activities that didn't appeal to her. If she felt she couldn't make a difference, she chose not to get involved.

Jackie considered many political events boring and a waste of her time. Frequently, she refused to attend recipe-swapping luncheons with Congressional wives or meet with the media. One of her biographers reported that she once told a friend, "Poor Jack, he thinks if I ignore them [the press], he'll be impeached." Jackie herself summarized her time as First Lady by saying, "People told me ninety-nine things I had to do as a First Lady and I haven't done one of them." Instead, she created her own road map because she knew where she wanted to go and how to get there.

After Jack Kennedy's assassination and Jackie's relocation to New York, President Lyndon Johnson offered her an ambassadorship to virtually any major country in Europe or Latin America. She recognized that there were other activities better suited to her than politics, and she declined his offer. Jackie consistently refused to take part in any activity where she would be less than the best.

Following the death of her second husband, Aristotle Onassis, she found herself at loose ends. Jackie wanted a purposeful life but wasn't sure exactly where to turn. Although Jackie had the intelligence, education, and energy to become a formidable businesswoman, she never set her sights on that. If she had, her skills in maneuvering around the dominant male species undoubtedly would have catapulted her into the board-room. When a friend suggested a job in publishing, she immediately recognized that this was well suited to her, as it was an arena where her natural gifts could be put to good use. After all, she had a lifelong love of learning and literature and had written poetry and essays throughout the years. She had also helped Jack organize and produce his Pulitzer Prize–winning book, *Profiles in Courage.* Additionally, she was primarily responsible for creating the White House guidebook and was fully familiar with all elements of the editorial process from editing the text to choosing the photos and designing the over-all layout.

Jackie took a job as a consulting editor at Viking Press and then at Doubleday, two of the country's leading publishers. Again, Jackie did it her way. She agreed to work three days a week in the office and the remainder of time from her home so she could be with her children. In short order, she gained the respect of her colleagues and authors, publishing more than seventy books during her tenure at Doubleday. From 1975 to 1994, for more than a third of her life, Jackie worked as a productive member of the publishing world. So successful was she that the *New York Times* dubbed her "Doubleday's secret weapon."

What Jackie Taught Us

Among the many lessons we can take from Jacqueline Kennedy's life is the necessity to believe passionately in what's important to us. This belief must be so strong that following it becomes as natural as breathing and ignoring it turns into something with which we cannot live. Jackie not only held on to her dreams, but she never looked to others to validate them.

Her highly developed sense of self served her well throughout her life. Rich or poor, famous or unknown, Jackie undoubtedly would have followed the same path she chose, as she knew which aspects of her life gave her joy and satisfaction and stayed close to them. In the words of the historian and teacher Joseph Campbell, "If you follow your bliss, you put yourself on a kind of track which has been there all the while waiting for you, and the life that you ought to be living is the one you are living." Obviously, Jackie followed her bliss.

She believed strongly in taking control of her life and spent time only on those things that truly mattered. Indeed, she could not visualize a life that didn't center around her core beliefs, which began with love of family, as well as that which nourished her soul—art, music, and literature. Finally, she possessed an overarching curiosity about the past that endowed her with a reverence for history and its reverberating truths for the present.

Jackie was always aware of what was important to her and what wasn't. Unlike those who lack self-awareness, she was able to realize her dreams because she gave great thought to what mattered most to her. The greatness of Jacqueline Kennedy's life is that she truly lived her beliefs until the end. And in doing so, she left the world a better place. As she so aptly characterized herself, "Maybe now people will realize that there was something under that pillbox hat."

Scheherazade

(EXCERPT FROM *COUNTRY GIRL: A MEMOIR*)

Edna O'Brien is the author of *The Country Girls*
trilogy and *Country Girl: A Memoir.*

$\mathcal{M}$Y PLAY *Virginia* was in rehearsal at the Public Theatre, and Kate Nelligan was asking me to take her through Virginia Woolf's last walk, across the fields in Sussex, before putting stones in her pockets to drown herself. A stagehand beckoned me aside to say there was a phone call from Jackie Onassis, but that most likely it was a hoax. It wasn't. There was Jackie at the other end of the phone, wondering if I had any time for her. I had, and so I was invited to dinner for the following evening. Her apartment was exquisite: there were modern paintings and sculptures, along with torsos and figurines from the ancient world. Jackie, feather-light, girlish, affectionate, capricious and willful, a Scheherazade who, instead of telling stories, encouraged them in others. That night, as she inquired into what I was writing and if the teaching curtailed it (which indeed it did), I remember her saying, "I want you to have a piece of the pie."

It amazed me that she would jog in Central Park, go to Morrissey's hair salon on Madison Avenue, walk all over without a bodyguard; but, as she said, sometimes people stopped her, though it was twenty years later, to tell her exactly what they were doing on that day in Dallas in November 1963. As I got to know her, I saw how she could do this, because of an instinctive gift to distance herself and, if necessary, to freeze someone out.

[One] evening in her apartment there was only us, as her companion, Maurice Tempelsman . . . had arranged to meet us later on in a restaurant. She spoke of the Kennedy men, the undoubted and inherited magnetism and their weakness, implicitly alluding to their infidelities, which she skimmed over. Mr. Kennedy Senior was not averse to touching her knee under the table, something her husband, even as President, was resentful of. The very first time she met Jack, she "fell," although she disguised the fact that she had fallen; she knew in her heart that by marrying him life would be a roller coaster, yet the alternative would be unthinkable.

After the President's assassination, Robert Kennedy was the one to keep her from falling apart, calling on her in her widowhood each evening, so much that many mornings she would find that his dog was outside her door, just like Argus, the dog in Homer, awaiting Odysseus, his master. She was at her most confiding and affectionate that particular evening. I was one of the three people on the planet whom she loved most. I said, how would it be, were she and I to fall in love with the same man, at which she remonstrated, said she would want me to have him, she would be my bridesmaid, but I did not believe her.

She was different from the other women, at once more amenable, more indiscreet, and yet aloof. She might grace this or that gathering, arriving like the costumed fairy who would mingle for a short while and then vanish. Her last letter to me, on notepaper the color of dark blue hyacinth, as she was dying, was full of hope, the spring, things we would do, life at full tilt again. It was not sentimentality; it was self-preservation. Long before she was a First Lady, she had the certainty of one who was cherished, and the little girl in her held on to that; it was her armor, and it saw her through varying nightmares with astonishing poise. Ironically, Marilyn Monroe, who in her sheath dress sang the birthday tribute for President Kennedy in 1962 (when Jackie was noticeably absent), had no sheath at all, the little girl in her had been cut to the core. Jackie was the opposite, she went through life veiled, and left it with her stardust intact.

Napoleon and Jacqueline

Dr. Andrew Roberts, FRSL, is the author of
*Napoleon and Wellington: The Battle of Waterloo—
and the Great Commanders Who Fought It* and
Waterloo: Napoleon's Last Gamble.

"S HE CREATED HER own road map because she knew where
she wanted to go and how to get there"

Reading this statement in Tina Santi Flaherty's *What Jackie Taught Us* brought to my mind the seemingly unlikely pairing of two extraordinary individuals: Jacqueline Kennedy Onassis and Napoleon Bonaparte, Emperor Napoleon I, who ruled over France from 1799 till 1815. The juxtaposition of these two lives perhaps seems more appropriate to me, as the author of two books on Napoleon, than others might suppose.

And while much—perhaps too much—has been made of Onassis's French heritage, there is no doubt that she shared a singular quality with Emperor Napoleon, which was aptly identified by Lady Jean Campbell in a wire to the London

Evening Standard at the time of President Kennedy's funeral: The First Lady had "given the American people from this day on the one thing they always lacked—*majesty*." And the kind of majesty that both Jacqueline and Napoleon exhibited had its roots in supreme self-awareness.

From a very young age, Napoleon had a very strong sense of what he was capable of achieving, derived from his fine French education in military academies that encouraged his fascination with the classics. In many people, self-awareness of the kind that equates oneself with the greatest men of ancient Greece and Rome—particularly Alexander the Great and Julius Caesar—might have been seen as a prima facie case of incipient lunacy. In Napoleon it was merely evidence of his acute sense of self—of his own thoughts, feelings, and abilities. For along with Alexander and Caesar, Napoleon did indeed turn into one of the seven great captains of warfare in the history of humankind. "In order to govern," he is quoted, "the question is not to follow out a more or less valid theory but to build with whatever materials are at hand. The inevitable must be accepted and turned to advantage."

Although Jacqueline Kennedy Onassis existed in a very different world, time, and sphere, there are connections between Napoleon's powerful sense of self-awareness and its benefits and Mrs. Onassis's. From her enduring legacy as First Lady to the passionate devotion in her post–White House years to her family, career, and causes, she turned her own self-awareness hugely to her advantage. As a result, she possessed a self-confidence that permitted her to achieve things that others—even those with apparently equal abilities—might have eschewed even the effort to try.

"I have been through a lot and have suffered a great deal," she said in candidly assessing her own life. "But I have had lots of happy moments, as well. Every moment one lives is different from the other. The good, the bad, hardship, the joy, the tragedy, love, and happiness are all interwoven into one single indescribable whole that is called life. You cannot separate the good from the bad. And perhaps there is no need to do so, either."

Self-confidence in those without the concomitant talents to justify it is mere vaulting ambition, a dangerous vice both for its possessor and for those who have to live with its consequences. Yet allied to talent, charm, intelligence, hard work, and other virtues—such as those that both Napoleon Bonaparte and Jacqueline Kennedy Onassis possessed in great measure—the self-confidence that springs from self-awareness can be one of the great naturally creative forces.

"She possessed an enormous inner strength and steely surety that had little to do with, it seems to me, where fate had brought her. Jackie, as I knew her, would have done just fine no matter where she landed."

—FRANK LANGELLA

WHAT JACKIE TAUGHT US ABOUT
Image and Style

THE POWER OF CHARISMA

"There can be no power without mystery. There must always be 'something' which others cannot altogether fathom, which puzzles them, stirs them, and rivets their attention."

—CHARLES DE GAULLE,
PRESIDENT OF FRANCE, 1958–1969

LIKE A COOL, cleansing breeze, Jackie Kennedy swept in and, overnight, changed the staid, conservative image of 1950s America into one of international style and elegance. When Jackie became First Lady, she quickly grasped that regardless of what she accomplished, she would be judged primarily by the way she looked. From her study of history and literature, Jackie knew that a carefully crafted image could be a powerful tool to project herself onto the world stage. Political and Hollywood personalities—and before them kings, queens, and prime ministers—have long used image as a vehicle to win followers and fans. Jackie was no exception, knowing exactly how she wanted to be perceived and directing everything toward it.

Through her unique image, Jackie was able to convey the possibilities and promises of the Kennedy presidential years to millions of people throughout the world. Even today, a magazine, photograph, history book, or video featuring an image of Jackie invariably triggers a poignant response upon seeing this vivid reminder of an era whose unfulfilled dreams were irretrievably lost.

To maximize her aura of style and glamour, Jackie accentuated her French heritage to the exclusion of her more dominant Irish roots. As her family name, Bouvier, was obviously French, it wasn't that much of a stretch. While ancestral blood does not predetermine success, Jackie's emphasis on her French background undoubtedly enhanced her image of elegance and sophistication in a manner that would not have been possible had she chosen to invoke the pastoral hills of Ireland that her mother's ancestors left in 1852.

Parental Influence on Jackie

Jackie's father, Jack Bouvier, endowed his daughter with more than just a French name. He taught her, by his own dashing style, that clothes do indeed make the man—or woman. Jack was an immaculate dresser whom women much admired for his style and panache. Jackie's mother, Janet, also wore expensive and sophisticated fashions, but she was more conservative and didn't have Jack's flair, except in her riding clothes. Jackie's parents, undoubtedly the people who were most influential in her life, gave her decidedly mixed signals about her ability to someday become a stylish, desirable woman.

Her father always seemed to delight in Jackie, telling her and anyone else in sight that she was a talented rider, not just winning first-place ribbons, but also was "the prettiest thing in the ring." He was so effusive in encouraging and praising his daughters, especially Jackie, that his family used to call it a dose of vitamin P—praise!

Her mother's attitude was just the opposite, frequently criticizing Jackie's appearance, possibly because her daughter's dark Mediterranean looks reminded her too much of the husband whose womanizing and fiscal irresponsibility were causing such unhappiness and despair. Listening to her mother, Jackie would hear that she was not feminine, unlike her fine-featured sister, Lee; that her hair was too frizzy; that her hands and feet (size 10) were too big; and that her shoulders were too broad and her hips too wide. In spite of these criticisms, Jackie's natural flair and style were destined to emerge. Her father's dashing example was too strong for her to ignore.

Janet and Jack Bouvier also offered Jackie intriguingly

dissimilar interpretations of style. Janet was rigidly, even obsessively, devoted to not standing apart in a crowd. Slavishly committed to an understated, almost dowdy interpretation of WASP style, she took great care to always dress appropriately, which for her meant rejecting bright colors and wearing instead beige, taupe, or off-white colors. She also preferred sensible shoes with medium heels and never wore pants unless it was jodhpurs for riding. Janet avoided form-fitting clothes, opting instead for a more relaxed style. She also used minimal makeup, which contributed to her rather bland appearance. Her hairstylist once told another client that Janet looked "like a mushroom" and he wished she would choose more colorful clothing. Janet was never gaudy or glitzy in her appearance, but she always insisted on having the finest quality in everything that she wore or touched. A simple lunch for herself at home would be served to her on a tray with linen, fine silver, and china.

Jack, often referred to as "Black Jack" because of his perpetual suntan, was the polar opposite of his wife in his sartorial tastes, striving always to be noticed and admired. Sporting a pencil-thin mustache on his handsome face, he was frequently photographed in his elegant clothing and often mistaken for the famous actor Clark Gable. He was so appealing that women couldn't resist his good looks, much to the chagrin of his wife, Janet.

Jack's clothes were always the best, including his tailor-made suits, shirts, and shoes. Even his ties were handmade to enhance the subtle shades of his suits. He skillfully managed to put everything together with highly distinctive and dramatic touches, resulting in a unique style that was both elegant and flashy. His dark complexion, carefully styled black hair, and piercing blue eyes added up to an exotic, almost forbidden, look.

Hope Annan recalled seeing Jack Bouvier at the fashionable Lawrence Beach Club, in Long Island, where her family were also members. "I was a young girl at the time, not even a teenager, but I remember how dashing he looked to me in the old-fashioned sense. He was handsome, full of self-confidence and charm and carried himself in a certain way. What struck me most was that his skin was so dark, it almost looked blue."

Jackie observed her father's success with the opposite sex and saw firsthand how clothes could be used to win admiration and even affection. In closely examining Jackie's fashion sense, a unique blend of upper-class restraint and cosmopolitan flair, it's likely that she was influenced by the distinctively different tastes of both parents. Jackie's own image of herself, a contradictory and complex mixture of her father's praise and her mother's scorn, also contributed to the development of her unique look. Many of her choices were defensive responses to Janet's criticism—such as the low-heeled shoes Jackie usually wore to disguise the size of her feet and the omnipresent gloves to hide her large hands and hard-bitten nails.

Black Jack continued to lavishly compliment his daughter on her good looks, helping to soften the blows of Janet's stinging criticism. His belief in Jackie's beauty must have helped her to realize eventually that despite her mother's negative appraisal, men found her attractive and desirable. Perhaps the mixed messages Jackie received from her parents led to the aura of mystery that she projected whenever she appeared in public. Her manner seemed to convey the message that, "You can look at me, but I don't want you to really know me," hinting that Jackie was afraid to let anyone discover the physical imperfections that her mother insisted she had.

A Woman for Her Time

Despite her mother's discouraging comments, as a young girl Jackie continually read fashion magazines, making little sketches and developing her own ideas about style. No doubt she was highly influenced by her interest in Europe, history, and the arts as well. By the time she became First Lady, she was poised and ready.

As writer Letty Cottin Pogrebin observed about Jackie, "Glamorous but no sex object, smart but no threat, she was the ideal transitional figure for that latent period between the passivity of the '50s and the revolutions of the '60s and '70s. Perhaps the only comparable public personality was Audrey Hepburn, who shared with Mrs. Kennedy aristocratic cheekbones, big dark eyes, and a soft breathy manner of speech. Girls with small breasts and respectable clothes could survive and flourish as long as Jackie and Audrey made the list of America's most admired women."

A passionate follower of fashion, Jackie continued to keep up to date with current trends, particularly those created by her favorite French designers. She knew exactly how she wanted to dress—regal without being fussy and, overall, to convey an aura of understated glamour that was not glitzy. She avoided anything décolleté or revealing to minimize her flat chest. Confident in her femininity, she felt no need to indulge in bosom-baring styles to prove it.

Her ramrod-straight posture, carefully honed through years of horseback riding, was a major asset, giving her a distinctive air of dignity. Suzanne Hemming, a special events producer remembers seeing Jackie at La Cote Basque, one of New York's most elegant restaurants and a favorite of discriminating diners. "I didn't go to Cote Basque that much but I had a client who wanted to try it," she said. "I had a good view of the front where the VIPs sat and I spotted Jackie, looking terrific as usual. I couldn't help but watch her when she ate. Even the way she lifted her fork was elegant. When she finished her meal, I'll never forget how she rose from the table, standing up in one solid movement. She stared straight ahead, pausing at the table until a waiter rushed over to pull it away from the wall. As she walked out, she reminded me of a ballet dancer, gliding off the stage. Her shoulders were back and yet down, her chest was up and her head had a slight upward tilt. She had no excessive movements, just very fluid and graceful. Everyone in the restaurant was mesmerized."

The Four Seasons, another elegant restaurant in Manhattan, was the scene of many Jackie sightings. Julian Niccolini, managing partner, vividly remembers the day he first met Jackie in the early 1980s in the restaurant's Grill Room—a favorite lunchtime gathering place for politicians and moguls, literary lions, and fashionistas.

"For as long as I live I will never forget the first time Mrs. Kennedy visited The Four Seasons Restaurant," says Julian. "It was just a regular day, a typical lunchtime scene. The Grill Room was packed and buzzing with the chatter of diners that included fashion designer Oscar De La Renta, *Vogue* editor Anna Wintour, real estate mogul Donald Trump and *W* magazine's founder, John Fairchild, among dozens of others."

Julian happened to look up and saw a lady quietly approaching him. "I couldn't believe my eyes when I saw it was Mrs. Kennedy. No one was expecting her. We had no reservation for her and I was awestruck."

Suddenly, the room went silent, recalls Julian. "Some of the most powerful men and women in America were stunned by her presence and in some cases stared at her with their mouths open. This had never happened at The Four Seasons before, or since. It was a once-in-a-lifetime experience that I don't think will ever be repeated."

Despite her dramatic arrival, Jackie simply smiled at Julian and whispered, "I am meeting a friend for lunch. I see him up there." Julian remembers being speechless and having no idea what to say. "Thinking about it after all these years still gives me the chills. It was profoundly unforgettable."

Years later, vivid memories of Jackie linger. "She was dressed beautifully, of course," the restaurateur said. "Someone told me it was a Valentino pantsuit. What I remember most about the occasion was how Mrs. Kennedy glowed. It was almost like she was lit from within with a kind of confidence and a certain charismatic love of life that I have never witnessed before."

Over the years, Jackie became a regular at The Four Seasons and always greeted Julian warmly. "When she arrived, she would whisper a friendly greeting to me, 'Hello Julian, so nice to see you,' in a quiet, kittenish purr that made me feel like I was the only man on Earth."

The Jackie Look

The clothing choices Jackie made, especially for her public appearances, reflected a conscious effort to convey the spirit of her husband's administration—youthful, but always with substance as its essence. Clean lines, solid colors, and ease of movement characterized her wardrobe. It was never her goal to set fashion trends. Bill Blass, the legendary American designer, paid Jackie the ultimate compliment when he said, "Jackie Onassis was the greatest pacesetter of our time—without doing anything highly original."

The "Jackie look" soon pervaded America: the pillbox hat, sleeveless A-line dresses, an Hermes scarf, Chanel-style suits, one-shouldered evening gowns, gloves, sari dresses, a double strand of faux white pearls, low-heeled pumps, and large, dark sunglasses.

Even her jewelry was imitated. Jackie didn't wear a lot of jewelry, but when she did she preferred the best, Van Cleef & Arpels and Tiffany and Co. among them. For daywear, she often wore her signature white pearls, which endowed her look with a ladylike finish. Pearls, whether real or fake, rapidly became a strong fashion statement for women across America.

In her formal wear, she usually avoided necklaces and sub-stituted large diamond earrings borrowed from one of the major jewelers who were eager to outfit her for the evening. She was an avid fan of master jeweler Jean Schlumberger, who designed exclusively for Tiffany. Knowing how much his wife admired the designer's jewelry, Jack thoughtfully gave Jackie a small, tasteful brooch of ruby strawberries with diamond leaves that he personally purchased for her. "Schlum," as Diana

Vreeland, the former editor of *Vogue* magazine and Jackie's fashion mentor, referred to the jeweler, also designed the colorful enameled bangle bracelets studded with gold that Jackie frequently wore. Extremely popular among ladies of style, they became known as "Jackie bracelets" and were eventually reproduced by various costume jewelers.

Choosing an "Official" Designer

During Jack's presidential campaign, Jackie's devotion to fashion became a political issue for a brief time after the Associated Press erroneously implied that she spent $30,000 a year on clothes, or about $184,000 in today's money. "I couldn't spend that much unless I wore sable underwear," was Jackie's response to *New York Times* reporter Nan Robertson. Seeing an opportunity to gain an advantage, the Republicans made a point of having Patricia Nixon, wife of presidential candidate Richard, talk about her love of American clothes purchased off the rack. Soon, the powerful International Ladies' Garment Workers Union, which had raised almost $300,000 for Kennedy's presidential campaign, began to pressure the Democrats to make sure that, if Kennedy won, Jackie's inauguration wardrobe would be made in America.

At this time, Paris was the indisputable heart of high fashion and home to some of the world's leading clothing designers, as New York City, London, and Milan had yet to emerge as fashion centers. Paris was where sophisticated women, including Jackie, preferred to shop. Understanding that her Francophile tastes in clothing designers—Chanel, Dior, and Givenchy—would likely harm Jack's presidential bid, Jackie quickly switched her allegiance to the American designer Oleg Cassini, who was also a Kennedy family friend. He became the official couturier for the White House and dressed Jackie for many of her most important political appearances.

By that time, Cassini, who was born a count in Paris, France, was one of the country's foremost fashion designers. His family had been forced to flee during the Russian Revolution and he and his brother, Igor, who later became the famed society columnist "Cholly Knickerbocker," grew up among the displaced "best families" of Europe.

After his training under the great French couturier Jean Patou, Oleg set sail for America. Arriving practically penniless in 1936 with a title, a tuxedo, and a tennis racquet, he became an American citizen six years later. His success as a leading costume designer for some of the major Hollywood studios and his marriage to the beautiful actress Gene Tierney brought him to the attention of Joe Kennedy, who recommended his services to daughter-in-law Jackie.

Choosing an official couturier was a difficult decision for Jackie, as not every American designer had the fashion sensibilities and elegance of manner she felt were important. Cassini's

training under Patou, plus his noble pedigree, uniquely quali-
fied him for the post.

According to Cassini, "One of the reasons President Kennedy was particularly comfortable with me was that I had
been a volunteer in the U.S. Cavalry. I spent five years in service and this was very important to him. He was Navy and I
was Army. Jackie also trusted me because she knew I'd never
take advantage of my position. I was honored that both Jack
and Jackie accepted me as a friend as well as a working professional." In a letter written to Cassini shortly after the inauguration, Jackie told him how pleased she was with his sketches
and that she was "proud to have you, a gentleman, doing clothes
for the wife of the President." Ending it with the customary
thoughtfulness she expressed to those whom she felt had done
a good job for her, she told Cassini that "If I look impeccable
for the next four years everyone will know it is you . . . Please
plan to stay for dinner every time you come to D.C. with
sketches . . . XO . . . Jackie."

During Jackie's thousand days as First Lady, Cassini
designed three hundred outfits for her, including some of the
most beautiful dresses she wore in the White House as well as
on her famous trips to Paris, Vienna, and India. From the
unforgettable fawn-colored wool coat ensemble with sable collar and muff, topped with a matching wool hat that she wore
when her husband was inaugurated, to the Grecian-style

moss-green gown she wore for the White House dinner honoring Nobel Peace Prize winners, the designer never let Jackie down. With Cassini discreetly in her corner, Jackie's impeccable taste and unerring fashion sense made an impact on style that has yet to be supplanted.

When Jackie became First Lady, Americans were not quite sure what to make of this young, stylish woman who stood in such sharp contrast to the grandmotherly images of her immediate predecessors Mamie Eisenhower and Bess Truman. Jackie's impeccable taste, however, soon dispelled any doubts. It's been said that Jackie's clothes did not wear her but she wore them—the ultimate accolade for a woman's fashion sense. Perhaps one of the reasons this was possible was because Jackie left nothing to chance. Prior to her triumphal visit to Paris in 1961, she sent a lock of her hair beforehand so the hairdresser would be able to create a suitable style for the upcoming dinner de Gaulle gave for the Kennedys at Versailles. Often she would "test-drive" a new outfit by wearing it to a private event before wearing it in public. For example, the never-to-be forgotten classic Chanel-style pink suit and pillbox hat Jackie was wearing in Dallas on the day of her husband's assassination was "tested" several days earlier when she wore it to Caroline's play group. Deciding that the outfit worked, she incorporated it into her official wardrobe. Sadly, the bloodstained pink suit became a ghastly symbol of that terrible day.

Oversized Sunglasses and Silk Scarves

Unlike most American women at the time, Jackie had discovered the particular power of accessories, using them to add verve and glamour to her look. Letitia "Tish" Baldrige, a friend from their teenage years at Miss Porter's school and who later became her White House chief of staff and social secretary, remembers, "Even then, she always had a deft way of wearing her clothes. She could put on a beret the right way while the rest of us would put one on and look like someone's cleaning lady trying to cover her hair. She knew how to tie a scarf in a chic way, and it would stay there. We'd try to copy her, and the knot would end up down our back."

Undoubtedly, the time Jackie spent in France as a college student also taught her how chic Parisian women could successfully accessorize an outfit using distinctive scarves, belts, and pocketbooks to add dash and style to an outfit, giving it dozens of different looks. Jackie's ultimate fashion accessory, however, was her dark, oversize sunglasses that covered her wide-set eyes, along with a silk scarf that she often wore wrapped around her hair, knotted under her chin, then tied in back. No one but Jackie could have made this hooded look appear so chic.

Her Perfect Choices

Whatever Jackie wore, it was invariably perfect for the occasion. She rarely appeared in black, usually choosing white, pastels, or a strong color instead. She had an uncanny ability to choose colors that were not only appropriate to the environment, but also made a strong visceral connection with her audience. Prior to the Kennedys' state visit to Canada in May 1961, the Canadian Ambassador paid a visit to Tish Baldrige and cautioned her, "We Canadians don't show our emotions. Even the Queen of England was very upset when she came, because she was used to an enthusiastic reception everywhere she visited in the British Empire. So please tell your President and First Lady that the unemotional response they will receive does not at all represent the Canadians' true feelings about their visit."

The Ambassador obviously underestimated Jackie's charisma and the excitement she invariably created. From the moment Air Force One set down in Ottawa, the Canadians went wild with enthusiasm. Cheering crowds lined the roads into the city and shouted "Jackie! Jackie! Jackie!" Cassini came up with a trim red wool suit and a matching pillbox hat that vividly echoed the scarlet uniforms of the Royal Canadian Mounted Police. This deliberate color choice was intended as a subtle compliment to the Canadian people, who prided themselves on the colorful appearance of their Mounties on horseback. The red suit was also a wise choice, as the design, although youthful, was still elegant. The clean lines of the suit shaped Jackie's body, emphasizing her trim figure. It was at this time that President Kennedy realized for the first time what an asset Jackie was. According to Oleg Cassini, "He was proud of her. I saw it in his face. She was Ambassador Numero Uno."

It wasn't until her trip to Paris in the same year that Jackie emerged as a worldwide charismatic figure, with her impeccable sense of style and glamour taking hold on an international scale. Jackie was extremely selective as to which political trips she would take with her husband. She had agreed to go to France with Jack for his meeting with General Charles de Gaulle partly because she loved Paris and partly because she knew Jack was uneasy about seeing de Gaulle after the Bay of Pigs fiasco, the failed attempt by the United States to oust Fidel Castro from Cuba. Jackie's unofficial role was to serve as goodwill ambassador and to help bridge the gap between de Gaulle and her husband, who thought that the General would be difficult to talk to.

No one could have predicted the impact she would make on the normally blasé French people. During the motorcade from Orly Airport to the city, more than a half-million spectators lined the roadways enthusiastically shouting, "Vive Jacqui!" much to the amazement of her husband and his political advisers. Never before had an American president's wife been so well received.

De Gaulle, a tall, imposing, and self-centered individual, did not easily warm up to people. Jackie, seated next to him during lunch at the Elysee Palace, completely charmed him, speaking in French about the history, arts, and culture of the country. "My grandparents were French," she proudly told him. "So were mine," he replied. Some noticed that de Gaulle was so taken with Jackie that he barely touched his food. He told President Kennedy, "Your wife knows more about French history than most French women." "And men," quipped Jack Kennedy.

The entire visit was a personal triumph for Jackie, topped off by a state dinner in the Hall of Mirrors at Versailles. "That night Jackie abandoned her all-American wardrobe and appeared in yet another awesome hairdo and bell-skirted gown—the supreme creation of French designer Hubert de Givenchy," gushed *Time* magazine. Featuring an embroidered bodice of lilies of the valley, it was interspersed with full-blown dark pink roses and other pastel flowers. The dress, evoking both youth and glamour simultaneously, was a sensation. According to Cassini, Jackie's choice of Givenchy was a special gesture to the French couture. He explained that "Jackie was terribly thoughtful and sweet to call me to explain why she felt, for political reasons, that she had to wear a French dress." Alexandre, a celebrated hairstylist in Paris at the time who told Mrs. Kennedy, "Madam, I will dress you like a queen," coifed her hair. He accomplished this by designing a bouffant style reminiscent of that worn by the Duchesse de Fontanges, one of Louis XIV's mistresses. Jackie's hair was held in place by diamond clips borrowed from the jeweler Van Cleef & Arpels. Finally dressed, Jackie and the President made their entrance into Versailles to the accompaniment of forty trumpeters in full eighteenth-century dress.

Jackie's emphasis that evening on all things French was not limited to her hair and gown. She even translated some of de Gaulle's remarks at dinner for Jack, who was clumsy with foreign languages. Jack himself was swept away into a new appreciation for his wife, and believed that because of Jackie's influence, de Gaulle was less hostile than he had expected. Her triumph was forever acknowledged when Jack rose to speak at a press luncheon for French journalists. "I do not think it altogether inappropriate to introduce myself to this audience," he declared. "I am the man who accompanied Jacqueline Kennedy to Paris and I have enjoyed it."

The world press declared the Kennedys' trip a stunning success, but it was Jackie who stole the show. "The radiant young First Lady was the Kennedy who really mattered," *Time* magazine reported. "Ravissante!" "Charmante!" "Apotheosis!" ran headlines in the French newspapers. In a little more than one hundred days since her husband was inaugurated President, Jackie had taken the world by storm. By the end of 1961, she had been voted "Woman of the Year" by one hundred international magazine editors.

The media couldn't get enough of Jackie, and ultimately her celebrity status brought her the kind of press attention she both loved and loathed. Knowing instinctively how to pose—a trait she most probably picked up from her photogenic father—Jackie was always ready for the camera with her broad smile, brightly focused eyes, and magnificently erect posture.

Although she clearly enjoyed this attention, she wanted it on her terms. Like many beautiful women who pride themselves on looking their best, she wanted to be photographed only when she so chose. That definitely did not include her private life or that of her family. There is no doubt that she despised the continual attention given her by the paparazzi who stalked her every step, whether she was eating an ice-cream cone on the street or taking her children to school. While it was clear that Jackie wanted to maintain her privacy, she was not against publicity. She simply wanted to control and use it as she saw fit.

In 1962, Jackie made a tour of India and Pakistan without the president. However, it was no ordinary goodwill trip for Jackie. Just three weeks earlier, anti-American feelings had erupted across India following stern U.S. criticism of India's invasion of Goa, a tiny Portuguese colony located on the west coast of the country. Prime Minister Nehru of India was furious, especially after the United States had hinted that it might halt aid to his country.

Prior to her departure, Jackie's press secretary had

announced, "This is Mrs. Kennedy's first semi-official trip by herself. She feels, and hopes, that it will be more memorable than just a group of fashion stories." As might be expected, though, Jackie's request was completely ignored and the press turned her every move into a dazzling photo opportunity, describing in great detail her clothing for each occasion. As she had carefully thought out her wardrobe well ahead of time, Jackie shrewdly wore the spectacular colors associated with India—strong pinks, canary yellows, ice blues, apricots, lavenders, and cool greens. She also included ivory, a color that would distinguish her among the colorful saris the other women were wearing. According to one reporter's account, during her two-week trip, she wore more than twenty-two different outfits.

When her plane landed at New Delhi and she emerged, all eyes were directed at Jackie, who was an incandescent vision in hot pink. She wore a stylized interpretation of a traditional rajah coat, a style also worn by Nehru and other men in India. Designed by Oleg Cassini, Jackie's outfit was topped with a Halston straw hat, also in hot pink, with matching grosgrain ribbon. It was well known that she utilized many aspects of a country's culture, history, and art to plan her wardrobe for these state visits. Most likely the outfit Jackie chose for her arrival to meet Nehru was a subliminal reaching-out on her part to demonstrate U.S. solidarity with India, its longtime friend. Upon seeing her, Nehru, who had become smitten with Jackie during his earlier visit to the United States, broke into a wide grin. So striking was her outfit that John Kenneth Galbraith, the U.S. ambassador to India, described Jackie as "looking like a million dollars in a suit of radioactive pink."

Jackie's official clothes were specifically designed for maximum photographic appeal so she would stand out in a crowd. During a visit to a Benares silk factory, Ambassador Galbraith said, "With her excellent sense of theatre, J.B.K. had put on a lavender dress which could be picked out at any range up to five miles." For a daytime boat ride on Lake Pichola to the maharana of Udaipur's palace, Jackie choose a rich, elegant dress and coat in apricot silk by Cassini. Although it was a formal design easily appropriate for a cocktail party, the rigid fabric held up beautifully in the stifling heat of India. The brilliant color and lustrous sheen of her ensemble made Jackie recognizable immediately to crowds standing on the far slope.

Jackie usually preferred solid colors and had a particular dislike of prints. In a rare departure, she chose a pointillist pattern in scarlet, orange, and hot pink for a dress and coat to wear on a camel ride in Karachi during a brief trip to Pakistan immediately following her visit to India. Seen at a distance, the tiny dotted pattern blended into a solid, brilliant hue that was more intense than any solid color could attain.

Early in the trip, Ambassador Galbraith had been concerned that the questions asked during a press briefing concentrated too much on Jackie's clothes, ignoring the political significance of her trip. However, by the end of her tour he readily agreed that Jackie's visit had been helpful for Indian-American relations. "[Nehru] was greatly attracted by Jackie," said Galbraith, "and this led to a more amiable view of the U.S. without much doubt." Jackie's effect on Nehru, who was completely enchanted by her, was obvious. Just as her father predicted many years earlier, men would not be able to resist her.

Speak Softly . . .

Apparently Jackie never forgot how elegant the women in India looked in their diaphanous saris gracefully draped across the contours of their bodies. Extremely feminine, this flattering garment is both demure and seductive at the same time. Jackie decided that the style also suited her. A friend of Jean Kennedy Smith, Jackie's sister-in-law, remembers seeing Jackie wearing a sari at a party held in the Smith townhouse in Manhattan. "My husband and I were invited to a Christmas party by Jean and Steve Smith in the early '80s. It was very cold outside and I wore a fancy, black velvet dress and my husband wore a tuxedo. Jean had put candles all over the house—on the mantle, up the stairs, and on all the coffee tables. I remember walking up the steps, past this wonderful Picasso painting and into a large, crowded living room. Suddenly Jackie walked in. Everyone stopped talking and all eyes were on her. She stood tall and erect, wearing a long sari with lots of fabric that

draped practically to the floor. I'll never forget the color—
turquoise and cream flecked with gold. She actually shim-
mered. All I could think of was how dramatic she looked. Here
I was in my safe, little black dress, just like half the women in
the room were, and Jackie had the self-confidence to wear a
thin, cotton, pastel sari in the dead of winter.

"When I was introduced to her, she spoke very softly, and
slowly, and enunciated every word, especially her vowels. It
almost sounded like 'How do-o-o you do-o-o?' When she lifted
her hand to shake mine, all I could think was that her sari was
going to catch fire, as she didn't seem to notice the candles when
she was moving her arm. I know it sounds dramatic, but some
people believe that the Kennedys are star-crossed, and I was
afraid the house was going to burn down with all of us in it."

Marlene Strauss, a former Vassar classmate of Jackie's and
now an art historian, was also struck by the distinctive quality
of Jackie's voice. "Before French class, we used to sit and talk
on the steps of Rocky, a building named after the Rockefellers.
Jackie and I would usually chat for a few minutes—nothing
personal, just a friendly exchange. Even then, she had an aura
about her that made you realize she was someone special. I'll
never forget the quality of her voice. It was soft, gentle, and
very sweet. It fascinated me. She never rushed her words. The
other girls at Vassar didn't sound like her."

Jackie's enduring image, however, goes far beyond fashion.
Her incomparable style influenced everything she did—the

people she chose to spend time with, the way she entertained, the books she read, how she handled key events in her life, and, of course, the manner in which she brought up her children. Her wit, her exquisite manners, and her acute intelligence were all part of her style. As the legendary designer Coco Chanel said, "Elegance is not limited solely to a woman's wardrobe. It is as much the way she conducts herself and her way of life."

Jackie's Influence on Culture

Jacqueline Kennedy is widely credited with revolutionizing the taste of America. As Diana Vreeland said in her autobiography *DV*, Jacqueline Kennedy "put a little style into the White House and into being First Lady of the land, and suddenly 'good taste' became good taste. Before the Kennedys, good taste was never the point of modern America—at all. The Kennedys released a positive attitude toward culture, toward style . . . and we've never gone back."

Undoubtedly, Jackie's charisma was a key factor in helping her achieve her ambitious goals. The successful restoration of the White House, as well as the cultural revolution she set in motion, were a direct result of her ability to persuade people to do extraordinary things that otherwise would never have occurred to them. Her cousin, John H. Davis, described her as possessing "a mysterious authority, even as a teenager, that would compel people to do her bidding."

Jackie's air of mystery also contributed to her appeal. She made herself available to a comparative few, rarely revealed her personal feelings, and never made her private pain public. Her insistence on privacy and the fact that her life was her own— not the public's—only added to her allure. As she accepted few invitations, her presence became all the more desirable. Davis also said that while Jackie outwardly seemed to conform to social norms, she had a "fiercely independent inner life which she shared with few people which would one day be responsible for her enormous success."

During the time of Jackie's tenure as First Lady, the press considered the personal lives of the President and his family off-limits and sacrosanct. Reporters were much more circumspect than in the post-Watergate days, when everything became fair game. Jackie was such good copy that reporters went out of their way to make her look good in their newspapers. Although Jackie was a chain smoker, she rarely was photographed with a cigarette in her hand.

In hindsight, it may be better that we don't know each and every detail of Jackie's life. Had she revealed more, perhaps we would have found a reason to admire her less. Ultimately, what Jackie did share with us was sufficient to forever ensure her place in our minds and hearts.

In a survey conducted by the Harris Poll in 2003, participants were asked which of the nine women who have served as First Lady since 1960 "will be viewed as the best First Lady by history." Of the 2,394 participants, Jacqueline Kennedy won the top place by overwhelming majority. Additionally, she was the leading choice as the First Lady who "best represented the United States with the rest of the world" and was also selected as "the best role model for women in America" by a wide margin.

It is fairly safe to conclude that Jackie's image as America's "best" will forever go unchallenged. It would be difficult, if not impossible, for anyone to ever seem that close to perfect again.

What Jackie Taught Us

Through her skillful use of image and style, Jackie made the world fall in love with her. But she was willing to work at it every day. How many of us give serious thought as to how we want to be perceived and then are willing to spend the necessary time to achieve it? Admittedly, Jackie had the money to dress well, but we all know that money doesn't buy good taste. Rich or poor, she would have found a way to look her best because it mattered to her.

Jackie knew that instant judgments are made about one's social status, wealth, and level of education based on appearance. It was from her parents that Jackie learned the importance of always looking her best, no matter what the occasion might be. Knowing that her clothing, jewelry, makeup, and hair sent out a strong message about who she was and what she stood for, she left little to chance.

Trends and fads never dictated Jackie's fashion choices. Even if a particular style was considered fashionable, she had the courage of her convictions to reject it if she didn't feel it was right for her. Jackie never permitted herself to be talked into anything she had the slightest doubt about. Each of us knows what works best for us if we let our inner voice guide us.

The old adage "less is more" always worked for Jackie. Her manner of dressing was restrained and simple, conveying the feeling that she never tried too hard. If you examine some photos of her in formal dress, you'll note that Jackie wore minimal jewelry. If she was wearing large earrings, she frequently omitted a necklace. She wore one ring or two, never three or four. At times she downplayed her jewelry, with her famous pearl necklace often inside her collar and the beautiful red ruby strawberry brooch that Jack gave her half hidden under her jacket. She wanted her jewelry to be tasteful and discreet, not overwhelming.

When it came to her wardrobe, Jackie was never stuck in the past. She realized when it was time to move on and put aside her white gloves, stiffly constructed day dresses, and matching pillbox hats. The more casual pantsuits and soft, silk shirts she wore in her later years reflect this. She appreciated the difference between what is timeless and what's temporary.

But Jackie's style encompassed far more than the clothing she wore; it also included the way she led her life. She made a conscious effort to treat everyone with equal grace and dignity.

A true superstar, Jackie never pulled rank, and she treated every doorman, housekeeper, and waiter the way she wanted to be treated herself. She was never considered rude even when confronted by aggressive strangers with intrusive questions and unwanted attention. She just smiled and moved on.

How we look, talk, and act speaks volumes about us, but it's how we treat others that says even more. The old truism, "perfection is made up of many trifles, but perfection is no trifle," was the song of Jackie's life. She is an icon and an example for all of us not only because she dressed beautifully, but because she also behaved beautifully.

Style and Substance

Hank O'Neal is a photographer and the author of *Berenice Abbott: American Photographer* and *XCIA's Street Art Project: The First Four Decades*.

*I*T WAS ALL because of a once-obscure but now celebrated turn-of-the-century French photographer named Eugène Atget that I first met Jacqueline Kennedy Onassis and was ultimately able to photograph her.

Atget was rescued from the dustbin of history by Berenice Abbott, an American photographer of some renown in her own right, who brought his negatives and prints to the United States in the late 1920s. She labored for forty years to establish his reputation.

In 1976, I began collaborating with Berenice on a book that would present a selection of her work, in particular her black-and-white photographs of New York City architecture and urban design of the 1930s. However, after almost three years, the project was floundering, along with the fortunes of

Horizon Press, the publishing house that had commissioned the book.

It was in November of 1979 that Mrs. Onassis came into our lives—and to our rescue. At the time she was on the board of the International Center of Photography, and Cornell Capa, founder of the ICP, suggested that the most celebrated member of his board might possibly sponsor Berenice's book at Doubleday, where she was employed as an editor.

I was aware that Mrs. Onassis had a lifelong interest in photography that began even before her first job as the Inquiring Photographer for the *Washington Times-Herald* in the early 1950s. And I knew that she was familiar with Atget's work because she had recently published and written the introduction for *Atget's Gardens*, a book about the deteriorating parks in turn-of-the-century Paris.

If nothing else, I guessed that she would be happy to talk about Atget with someone like Berenice, who had such intimate knowledge of the enigmatic Frenchman. But at our first meeting, it was clear that Mrs. Onassis was taken with Berenice and her work, which embodied two of Mrs. Onassis's passions: historic preservation and photography.

About a month after our meeting, Mrs. Onassis asked to come to my place to look at all the Abbott photographs I'd assembled. After a few hours going over them, she spent time looking at the other photographs hanging on my walls.

Mrs. Onassis was particularly impressed with a sixteen-by-twenty-inch photograph I'd printed from one of the Atget glass plates still in Berenice's possession. She'd never seen anything by Atget except smaller contact prints or reproductions in books and was astounded by how good this one looked enlarged—and was equally engaged with the technical aspects of how I achieved such a fine-quality enlargement.

When she asked if she could borrow my copy of *Atget Photographe de Paris*, the first book about him, I replied, "Of course. And you can keep it as long as you like, if you'll let me take a photograph of you holding it." Without hesitation she agreed, and we headed to the room I use as a studio.

My old five-by-seven-inch Deardorff was already set up under a large skylight. With very little fuss on her part, I made three one-second exposures. It was over in a few minutes.

The portrait shows a strong and confident woman. She is very glamorous in her elegant knee-length mink coat and long scarf tied in a stylish knot, but in an understated, sophisticated way. Nothing is forced; this was just the way she was on a day in December 1979, projecting an elegant image into a very old-fashioned camera. No tricks, no elaborate lighting, no effects. In all likelihood this is one of the few, if not the only, formal, large-format post-1963 photograph of one of the most photographed women of the last century.

Unfortunately, the book of Berenice's photos didn't work out at Doubleday. According to Mrs. Onassis the company insisted that the book be printed at their own facility. She didn't think this option would offer the best results and said she'd find us another publisher, which she did. But Mrs. Onassis continued to be a presence in our lives.

At an International Center of Photography tribute to Berenice, which took place at the top of the World Trade Center, Mrs. Onassis spent the better part of the evening watering Berenice's wine with ice cubes, so the guest of honor would keep her face out of her plate. I like to think that it was just one of the many subtle ways in which she supported the arts, literally.

The last time I saw her was on the evening of November 19, 1991, at a gala held at the Henri Bendel store to benefit the Municipal Art Society, a nonprofit organization dedicated to preserving some of what Jackie loved best about New York—its historic landmarks, architecture, and public spaces. My father-in-law, Harry Shier, whose company provided fixtures for the refurbished store's interior, had purchased a table for family members.

The Municipal Art Society was represented by Mrs. Onassis and author Brendan Gill, who were both board members of the organization. It turned out that protocol dictated that each of them shake hands with all three hundred guests—before anyone could be fed. The line moved along at a pretty rapid pace because the handshakers were on automatic.

When my turn finally came, Mrs. Onassis—still very much on automatic—stuck out a gloved hand, then looked up and, very surprised, said, "Hank, what are you doing here?" We chatted for a few moments about this and that. Meanwhile, my Canadian in-laws looked on in amazement. I had always been suspect with this rather reserved lot as I was a product of the east Texas Bible Belt. I am sure they thought I'd lived in a tar-paper shack without running water and eaten dirt as a child. But this simple handshake and a short conversation elevated my reputation considerably.

Over the years, Mrs. Onassis and I had continued to talk about books and photography. The last letter I received from her, dated February 6, 1992, is kind and to the point, offering a suggestion on a book project. She signed it "Jackie."

Jackie O

C. D. Greene is a fashion designer.

"In 1951, Vogue *awarded its coveted Prix de Paris junior editorship to a graduating senior from George Washington University. Appearing in the August 15 issue is a portrait [by Richard Rutledge] of the chosen: She is a raven-haired beauty, sitting erect, white-gloved hands perfectly crossed; a double strand of pearls, hung with a four-leaf clover, echoes the softly rounded lines of her face; above a Mona Lisa smile, her wide-set, leonine eyes gaze confidently—challengingly, even—into the photographer's lens."*

—VOGUE

THROUGHOUT HER LIFE, Jacqueline Kennedy Onassis evoked an effortless style, whether as a student and young career woman, First Lady, or during her many years living and working in New York. As a public figure, she was very conscious of the impact of how she looked and what she wore would have not only on her own image but on the presidency and the nation that she represented. As a private citizen who was still the subject of close attention from the media and the public, she never lost her poise and elegance, no matter how informal the occasion, how casual her dress, or how unexpected an encounter with the paparazzi. She never looked uncomfortable or out of place.

Even though it has been more than fifty years since she and President Kennedy occupied the White House, it is the image of this handsome young couple that has endured. And most especially the image of Jackie—the striking, slender brunette, with her, "wide-set, leonine eyes" and her confident— challenging, even—gaze.

In 2004, when I was home in Chicago for Christmas, I attended the exhibit "Jacqueline Kennedy: The White House Years," which was then at the Field Museum of Natural History. This collection of "some 80 original costumes and accessories" reminded me of how exacting she was in selecting her wardrobe, taking into account the kind of event or place where she would appear.

The exhibit's press materials declared, "According to [Hamish] Bowles [then European editor-at-large of *Vogue* and creative consultant to the exhibition] the costumes vividly illustrate that, as First Lady, Jacqueline Kennedy's personal style choices were to prove a visual metaphor for her cultural aspirations for the White House. Under her aegis, it would become an exquisite and stylish showplace, and a background for a worldly and sophisticated mix of guests drawn from the realms of arts and culture as well as national and world politics and diplomacy."

Because I'm a lifelong Jackie fan, it's no surprise that when I think of great women who have influenced me in my fashion collections, she always comes to mind first. There is always a little bit of her in every collection.

Jackie's choices were always fashion forward but appropriate for the time and the venue. As the 1960s came to a close, she retired the pillbox hat and gloves, creating her own interpretations of current styles. As she grew older she favored the classics—slacks, silk blouses, and sweaters for every day—simple, elegant, and understated. And yet, she still maintained an aura of glamour and mystery with her signature oversize sunglasses and chic silk scarf covering her dark hair. Perhaps she thought of these as a disguise, but she was still instantly recognizable to almost every passer-by as she made her way around the streets of Manhattan or strolled through Central Park.

"In a time of gilt and glitz and perpetual revelation," wrote Anna Quindlen in the *New York Times* shortly after Jackie's death, "she was perpetually associated with that thing so difficult to describe yet so simple to recognize, the apotheosis of dignity."

What a wonderful legacy of style, grace, *and* dignity Jackie left for all of us!

What Jackie Taught Us About
Vision

LISTENING TO YOUR INNER VOICE

"Your vision will become clear only when you look into your heart."

—CARL JUNG

To many people, Jackie will be remembered forever as America's queen, an icon and a touchstone for the wistful remembrance of 1960s culture and the Camelot dream. Yet she easily could have been merely a famous footnote to her husband, accorded no more recognition than that of any presidential wife. Why and how did Jackie leave such an indelible mark?

It begins with the fact that Jackie had a vision for our nation to which she held fast and would not let go. Just as President Kennedy declared a goal for America to put a man on the moon, Jackie imagined a transformed White House, alive with history and culture, and restored to its former glory as the First House of the land.

Within each of us lies our own vision for the way we want to live our lives. Like Jackie, we must recognize and hold fast to our dreams and refuse to be discouraged. One of Jackie's favorite poets, W. B. Yeats, beautifully echoed these thoughts when he wrote,

> *I have spread my dreams under your feet;*
> *Tread softly because you tread on my dreams.*

Jackie was one of those rare individuals who completely trusted her inner voice without needing the approval of others. Even as a child, she was introspective and determined to discover her own answers. Once she found them, she was fully committed to her goals and could not be persuaded otherwise.

Transforming America's Image

Prior to Jackie assuming the role of First Lady, America was not thought of as particularly sophisticated in music, art, literature, or even the culinary arts. The presidency of Dwight D. Eisenhower and his wife, Mamie, had done little to change that. In fact, much of the civilized world deemed Americans uncouth and uneducated. Jackie personified the opposite and was the epitome of a sophisticated, cultured woman. Almost single-handedly, she transformed the way America was perceived—at home and abroad.

Through her unwavering support of the arts, Jackie demonstrated that America—although still culturally young by comparison with the rest of the world—produced poets, musicians, and other artists of incredible talent who could rival the world's best, and often did. Through her restoration of the White House, Jackie rekindled the nation's pride and appreciation for its historic beginnings and cultural heritage. While juggling all of this, she was still first and foremost a loving wife and a devoted mother whose destiny was to be a major player on the world stage.

Unlike present-day politicians who rely on opinion polls and surveys, Jackie didn't find it necessary to ask advisers what activity would be the most popular or appropriate. From the very beginning of her husband's presidency, she was set on restoring the White House, along with elevating the arts in America, and she directed all her energies toward making it a reality.

Jackie never forgot her first trip to Washington, DC, when she was eleven. Her mother brought her and her sister, Lee, to visit the Capitol and other sights during Easter week in 1941. Jackie's first visit to the White House, after waiting in a long line with other tourists, was a disappointment. "I felt strangely let down by the

White House. It seemed rather bleak. There was nothing in the way of a booklet to take away, nothing to teach one more about that great house and the presidents who lived there."

Restoration of the White House

In 1960, the executive mansion was little more than an amalgamation of poorly furnished rooms that did nothing to project the spirit of America and its courageous beginnings. When Mamie Eisenhower gave Jackie an introductory tour of the White House, the new First Lady was both shocked and offended by the dreary appearance of the interior. Jackie observed that the rooms where state functions were held were "tattered, worn, and seemed to have no rhyme or reason. I felt sad for the neglected rooms. . . . It disturbed me to know that these badly designed, poorly maintained rooms belonged to the United States. . . . What did the kings and queens and great statesmen of the world think when they came to our President's home?" With her passion for history and her innate appreciation of beauty and design, Jackie knew immediately what needed to be done.

Between the election and the inauguration, Jackie scrutinized history books and files on the White House supplied by the Library of Congress. "We must make this building something that they will be proud of. I want to make it the First House in the land."

In attempting to restore the 132 rooms of the White House, Jackie was taking on a daunting task—not only was it overwhelming in sheer size but fraught with political peril. The White House is a highly visible government property belonging to all Americans. Any alterations or changes could present serious political problems, which understandably concerned Jack Kennedy.

Initially, he was very much opposed to Jackie's plans and told her that he couldn't allow her to take on a high-profile redecoration that surely would bring about unwanted attention. Perhaps he was thinking about past presidents, including Martin Van Buren and Harry Truman, who had sought to make changes in the White House and in the process earned the ire of Congress as well as the public. Jackie was just as adamant, emphasizing to Jack that it wasn't a redecoration but a restoration.

Jack then asked Clark Clifford, his personal attorney and a trusted adviser, to intervene. After seeing that Jackie wouldn't be dissuaded, Clifford wisely suggested forming the Fine Arts Committee for the White House to provide legal and political cover. Its purpose would be to raise funds and solicit donations of historically correct furnishings, thereby deflecting any potential criticism that taxpayer money was being used frivolously.

Jackie's vision was so compelling that others were eager to

join with her to make it a reality. The Fine Arts Committee quickly came together, barely a month after the inauguration. Jackie's organizational talents emerged immediately. She personally persuaded the leading authority on early American furniture, multimillionaire Henry Francis du Pont, to chair the committee. Although he was a prominent Republican, Jackie chose him for his knowledge, not his politics. Du Pont's appointment virtually guaranteed acceptance and cooperation by wealthy, old-money patrons as well as by curators, collectors, and academics across the country.

Jackie had the unique ability to see each step she needed to take to reach her objective. She managed every detail of the restoration, ensuring that each room was restored with historical accuracy. She solicited contributors, kept warring curators from each other, and successfully urged donors to part with treasures from their personal collections. In a decided coup, she single-handedly persuaded Walter Annenberg, a wealthy media baron and major art collector, to give up his prized portrait of Benjamin Franklin to add to the White House collection. She also succeeded in retrieving Thomas Jefferson's inkwell and George Washington's armchair. Her confident style was fueled as much by her certainty of purpose as by her authority as First Lady.

Although outwardly the restoration appeared to be a team effort—with Jackie working with her impressive committee of wealthy, knowledgeable people as well as the curator and the official White House interior designer Sister Parish—there was no doubt that Jackie had the final say. Wisely she realized that if she were to achieve her vision, she should not compromise it, and she didn't hesitate to go to considerable lengths to have her way while trying to avoid political repercussions for Jack.

Jackie virtually hid the involvement of French designer Stephane Boudin, quietly brought in to add the authentic French sensibilities that, historically, some of the rooms required, and frequently ignored the wishes of committee chairman Henry du Pont—even after agreeing with him publicly. Eventually, this charade was uncovered by *Newsweek* reporter Maxine Cheshire, who described the restoration project as "a tale that encompasses scholarship, wrangling over prices, discreet pressure, petty jealousies, and a cast of influential characters who keep well behind the velvet curtain Jackie has drawn around the inner workings of her program."

A Vision Realized

Jackie accomplished the restoration in record time. In a little more than a year, she turned what was often referred to as the "Shabby House" into a magnificent mansion that proudly reinforced not only America's good taste, but also its historical role as the bedrock of democracy.

This amazing feat captured the image of her husband's

presidency in a way that is remembered until this day. Millions of Americans clamored to see what magic Jackie had wrought. On the night of February 14, 1962, more than fifty million viewers tuned in their television sets to watch *A Tour of the White House with Mrs. John F. Kennedy*. CBS newsman Perry Wolff, who wrote and produced the program, was very impressed by Jackie's knowledge of the various antiquities in the White House. "I had prepared a script for her which she had marked up. Although my research team was very careful about documenting the provenance of the various artifacts in the White House, Jackie immediately spotted some mistakes. She absolutely knew her stuff. She was amazing."

While millions of viewers at home saw the program, Wolff witnessed something else that few people saw. "After the taping was over, I showed President and Mrs. Kennedy a rough copy of the shooting in a private screening room at the White House. I sat directly behind the presidential couple. When the projection was finished, President Kennedy said, 'Mr. Wolff, Jackie was wonderful.' He was so proud of her and they actually beamed at each other. There was a quick little snuggle between them. I saw real love there. It was a very sweet moment."

According to the Museum of Broadcast Communications, this prime-time television documentary was the first in which a woman narrated large segments of the text, reflecting the emerging role of women in American society.

It was an evening of triumph for Jackie, with the television cameras following her from room to room as she told viewers about the transformation of their national home into a true museum with authentic furnishings and objects of great beauty. During the broadcast, Jackie discussed a previous visit she and the President had made to the Presidential Palace in Colombia, where every piece of furniture had some link with the past. "I thought the White House should be like that. It just seemed to me such a shame when we came here to find hardly anything of the past in the house; hardly anything before 1902. . . . I have always felt that American history is sometimes a dull subject. There's so much emphasis on dates. But I think if [young students] can come here and see . . . this building and—in a sense—touch the people who have been here, then they'll go home more interested. I think they'll become better Americans. Some of them may want to someday live here themselves—which I think would be very good."

Jackie, fully aware that previous presidents had decorated the White House according to their personal whims, was concerned that a future First Lady who didn't share her vision could possibly dismantle her work. She campaigned adroitly behind the scenes to solve this potential problem, and ultimately Congress gave the White House museum status with its contents fully protected. At the same time, a White House curator's office was established, providing additional long-term protection. In order to fund future acquisitions, Jackie produced a guidebook, *The White House: An Historic Guide*. To date, more than eight million copies have been sold.

Jackie was successful in restoring the White House because she had the confidence to respond decisively to her vision and the determination to overcome any major obstacles that arose. Beyond her iron will, superb organizational skills, and highly persuasive manner, she ultimately achieved her goal because she had chosen a project in which she completely believed. Throughout her life, she involved herself only in activities to which she was 100 percent committed and avoided the rest—a valuable lesson for all of us.

Unofficial Minister of Culture

After her successful restoration of the White House, Jackie turned to her goal of transforming the role of the arts in America, wanting to infuse Washington with the spirit and culture she had seen in cities like London and Paris. To many, she became the nation's unofficial Minister of Culture. This isn't so surprising, considering that from childhood on, Jackie was devoted to artistic endeavors—she wrote poetry, drew whimsical sketches, read classical literature, visited the world's great museums, and regularly attended musical and ballet performances.

The vehicle Jackie chose to showcase the arts was brilliantly simple. She began in the home where she and the President resided, the White House. According to Tish Baldrige, Jackie's chief of staff and social secretary, "The Kennedys made history with their after-dinner performances in the East Room. They proudly showed off the best of the best to the world." Wanting Americans to take pride in their cultural as well as their political heritage, Jackie invited prominent musicians such as the famed cellist Pablo Casals to perform. Internationally known composers, including Leonard Bernstein and Aaron Copland, led their orchestras in performance as well. The Kennedys were also the first to hold youth concerts that encouraged countless young people to appreciate music. Some of the world's greatest actors, including Basil Rathbone and Fredric March, recited excerpts from classic drama and fiction. After she left the White House, Jackie told the press, "President Kennedy and I shared the conviction that the artist should be honored by society, and all of this had to do with calling attention to what was finest in America, what should be esteemed and honored. The arts had been treated as a stepchild in the United States."

As it was in Jackie's artistic nature to put her personal stamp on everything she did, she radically altered the rules for White House state dinners. Envisioning entertaining in the newly restored White House as a performance on the world stage, she instinctively realized that these evenings were more than mere "entertainment." In a drastic change from previous administrations, the Kennedy dinners were replete with exquisite food, beautiful table décor, and stirring after-dinner performances by some of the country's outstanding musicians and actors.

These evenings demonstrated Jackie's discerning taste while echoing her belief that beauty mattered and that artistic achievement was important. These fabled dinners, still talked about more than forty years later, were a powerful image that projected to the world that America's intellectual and artistic community rivaled that of any of its European counterparts.

Pablo Casals's performance at the White House in 1961 made international headlines. The last time chamber music had been played with any frequency in the White House was during Thomas Jefferson's administration, almost 160 years earlier. Casals, then in his eighties, had not performed in America for more than thirty years, refusing to appear in any country that supported Spain's Francisco Franco. It's widely reported that Casals made an exception for the Kennedys because he admired the President's commitment to world peace. The *New York Times* reported that the Casals's concert "was much more than a mere evening of music. It was an indication that the White House is rising to its responsibilities and—in one respect, at least—coming of age."

At long last, Jackie's dream of making the White House America's premier bastion of culture was becoming a reality. The *New York Times* also reported that "it is felt by many creative figures in America that the interest in the arts displayed by the White House cannot help but spark an awareness from the public about the importance of culture in the American scheme of things."

As composer Leonard Bernstein vividly recalled the Casals's evening in his memoirs, "I couldn't help comparing it with the last time I had been at the White House, which had been during the reign of Eisenhower when I had played with about thirty members of my orchestra. To compare that dinner with the Casals dinner is to compare night and day. In the case of the Eisenhower dinner, it was very stiff and not even very pleasant, and the food was ordinary, and the wines were inferior, and you couldn't smoke. Compare that to the Casals's dinner. It's all like having dinner with friends. The food is marvelous, the wines are delicious, there are cigarettes on the table, and people are laughing, laughing out loud, telling stories, jokes, enjoying themselves, glad to be there. It was like a different world, utterly like a different planet."

Dark Days

As idyllic as that time was in the White House, it was soon to be followed by some of the darkest days in American history with the assassination of President Kennedy. As the nation mourned, it was Jacqueline Kennedy who led us through our grief. Jackie, who believed in the greatness of John Fitzgerald Kennedy's presidency, was determined that his funeral would reflect this and indelibly secure his legacy. Longtime White

House reporter Helen Thomas wrote, "Majestic in her sorrow, she honored John Fitzgerald Kennedy at a state funeral that will go down in American history for its grandeur and dignity."

Birth of Camelot

As Jackie began to focus on ways to immortalize Jack's memory, she realized that the assassination and its aftermath would occupy an important place in history. She resolved to have control over how it would be portrayed. Just four days after the funeral, Jackie telephoned journalist Theodore H. White from her home in Hyannisport, where she was spending a subdued Thanksgiving weekend, and asked him to meet with her there. She knew he was working on a piece about the assassination for *Life* magazine and saw an opportunity to have an impact on the author's words—the first step in her mission to create a unique history about Jack's presidency. Earlier, White had written *The Making of the President,* a book much admired by Jack.

After receiving her call, White had to make a quick decision. There was fog and heavy rain on Cape Cod, the magazine's deadline was only hours away, his elderly mother was ailing, and he was exhausted from covering the assassination and three days of the memorial service. But he agreed to travel that evening to see Jackie. He remembered being struck by her presence. No longer clad in the black widow's dress, Jackie wore a beige sweater, black trousers, and flats. "The chief memory I have of her is of her composure," he said, "of her beauty, her eyes wider than pools and of her calm voice and total recall."

Jackie was determined that White's portrayal of her husband would concentrate on his heroic characteristics, avoiding the gruesome details of the assassination. Despite what must have been the most painful week in her life, with the grief of mourning her husband and the sheer exhaustion of planning every detail of his funeral service, Jackie was completely focused on what she wanted to achieve that evening.

She told White that Jack, as a little boy, had been sick a great deal and had spent much time reading about the Knights of the Round Table and developed a sense of history that was filled with heroes and idealism.

In fact, she had created a magical context for Jack Kennedy's one thousand days in office—the legend of Camelot, taken from a song written for a hit Broadway musical that glorified the mythical kingdom of King Arthur and his knights. She told White that "at night, before going to bed . . . we had an old victrola, he'd play a couple of records . . . It was a song he loved, he loved Camelot. 'Don't let there be forgot that for one brief shining moment there was Camelot'. . . "

"She put it so passionately that, seen in a certain light, it almost made sense," said White. "I realized it was a misreading of history, but I was taken with Jackie's ability to frame the tragedy in such human and romantic terms. There was something extremely compelling about her . . . yet all she wanted was for me to hang this *Life* epilogue on the Camelot conceit. It didn't seem like a hell of a lot to ask. So I said to myself, Why not? If that's all she wants, let her have it . . ."

It was 2 o'clock in the morning by the time he had finished and handed the typewritten pages to Jackie. She made numerous changes, the most significant being the last line that she added: "For one brief shining moment there was Camelot."

In weaving the legend of Camelot into the fabric of her husband's presidency, Jacqueline Bouvier Kennedy was portraying John Fitzgerald Kennedy's time in office as akin to the era of the Knights of the Round Table—when courageous men performed noble deeds and their women, equally appealing, loved and honored them for it. It was a vision that cast a magical and enduring overlay on Jack Kennedy's presidency that remains to this day.

What Jackie Taught Us

Jackie was one of the fortunate few who dared to dream of a wider world. She looked beyond the immediate horizon and was able to imagine what she wanted and how to go about getting it. Her vision was never static. As life presented her with new opportunities, her vision changed with it.

Developing your own vision is not that difficult. If you know what you want to achieve and have an idea of how to go about it, you will not only be able to do it but to do it better than you ever thought possible. Jackie's vision for herself was uniquely her own and focused on what she wanted to accomplish as First Lady, as a wife and mother, and as an individual. She took charge of her vision and didn't let others dictate to her what it should be. We, too, should acknowledge that it's our personal vision that's important, not someone else's idea of what's best for us.

Jackie taught us to truly believe in our dreams, no matter how much others might try to discourage us. What she envisioned for the White House was clearly not what others could see or even wanted to see. It was a struggle to win over the hearts and minds of those around her, including her husband, but she kept on until she prevailed. From Jackie we learned that dreams alone are not enough. We must also develop a plan and have the will and courage to follow through.

Vision can be about the ordinary things in our lives as well as the monumental ones. Dreaming little dreams is as acceptable as dreaming big ones. Sometimes we may fall short in our quest to attain what we want, just as Jackie did when she failed in her initial attempts to convince Jack to marry her. But she held fast to her vision for a life with Jack, and eventually they married.

Although each of us has a personal vision of what we'd like our life to be and what we want to accomplish, there are many values and goals that we share with others. Jackie showed us the rewards and satisfaction possible from actively supporting the vision of those we love. Just as Jackie went to extraordinary lengths to help her husband succeed as president, we can offer the encouragement, knowledge, and talent to assist a family member or close friend to achieve his or her own dream.

In addition to family and friends, we can also derive much gratification and happiness from supporting the vision of outsiders. When Jackie joined the fight for the preservation of Grand Central Station and historic Lafayette Square in Washington, DC, she demonstrated that the seemingly impossible could be achieved if like-minded individuals pool their dreams.

Following your dream, which is really what vision is all about, is the essence of a meaningful and exuberant life. Each of us can succeed in achieving our vision, no matter what the odds. But even if we run aground, the rewards can be great. What we learn on one journey becomes the building blocks for the next. Jackie reached for a star and touched greatness. Each of us can find our own special star if we dare to dream!

A Lasting Achievement

Ashton Hawkins is the former executive vice
president and counsel to the trustees of the
Metropolitan Museum of Art.

*J*ACKIE KENNEDY ONASSIS returned to New York and her
apartment at 1040 Fifth Avenue across from the Metropolitan Museum in 1964. At about that time she became involved
with the Metropolitan, an institution she went on to serve without credit—as she always preferred—as an adviser, a supporter,
an author, and also a good friend. Perhaps her most lasting
achievement—largely unknown and described further on—
was the role she played in getting the Temple of Dendur to the
museum.

Jackie had always been particularly interested in the art of
ancient Egypt. She was well aware of the Metropolitan's ongoing effort to raise emergency funds for UNESCO to help save
important Nubian monuments that would otherwise be inun-
dated by the completion of the Aswan Dam. In 1962, she

successfully urged President Kennedy to get the United States to generously support UNESCO's fund. She also told me—years later—that in 1963 she received a photograph album from the State Department of the nine monuments to be saved and had been invited to choose one monument. She chose the Temple of Dendur, which was ultimately—after many difficulties—installed in the Metropolitan in 1979.

As I became a better friend of Jackie's and went to her parties, she took great pleasure in pointing out the Temple of Dendur from her apartment window. Yet, she never mentioned her role in choosing the temple.

But perhaps her most "glamorous" contribution was to the Metropolitan's Costume Institute. Since her time as First Lady, Jackie had been a good friend of Diana Vreeland, then the editor of *Vogue*. She had asked and received Vreeland's advice in regard to handling the many designers who were clamoring to be chosen by her.

After Vreeland had been forcibly retired by Condé Nast in early 1972, Thomas Hoving, the Metropolitan's director, met her for the first time. He immediately understood how she could be a valuable addition. On July 1, 1972, she was hired to become a special consultant to the Costume Institute, the most expansive collection of Western fashion history in the world. Both Jackie and Diana saw an opportunity to work together again.

Hoving and Vreeland had made a trip to Russia in early 1975 in search of rare and beautiful eighteenth- and nineteenth-century costumes hidden away in museums. On Hoving's second trip to Russia he invited Jackie to come with him. Her presence there created a great stir and helped ensure that the proposed exhibition would actually take place. When "The Glory of Russian Costume" opened in 1976, Jackie was the editor of the exhibition catalog. She later wrote a tribute to Vreeland as part of the catalog for another exhibition, "Vanity Fair," and continued for many years to contribute to and help support the Costume Institute.

Jackie had also become interested in the Metropolitan's Program for Art on Film, which was led by Karl Katz, a special consultant to the museum. Karl had hired Jackie's daughter, Caroline, to help structure the filming of selected exhibitions hosted by a curator and to be distributed to museums, universities, and educational programs on television. Jackie soon took on an important advisory role in Art on Film and also in later years chaired several fund-raising events for Art on Film at the Temple of Dendur.

In the early 1980s Jackie urged me to accept an invitation to become a trustee of the Municipal Art Society of New York. In sharing that interest we became even better friends. She had served on the board for quite some time and had played an important role when the MAS was supporting New York City's legal battle to save Grand Central Terminal, one of New York's most beautiful and historic public spaces, from demolition. She was a leader of the prominent delegation in 1978 that traveled by train to Washington to hear the Supreme Court decision that sustained the New York City landmark law and thereby saved Grand Central.

In the fall of 1993, Jackie invited me to escort her to the hundredth-anniversary celebration of the Municipal Art Society, which was held in Vanderbilt Hall in Grand Central Terminal. She was exceptionally outgoing, proud, and happy that evening and she helped make it a memorable event for everyone there.

When Jackie died of cancer on May 19, 1994, all of America came together to mourn her death. Seven years later the Metropolitan Museum and its director, Philippe de Montebello, were proud to celebrate her life with a memorial exhibition: "Jacqueline Kennedy: The White House Years."

"As we strive to fulfill our vision, we must make the most of every living moment."

—JAQUELINE KENNEDY ONASSIS

What Jackie Taught Us About

Courage

THE ABILITY TO BEND, NOT BREAK

"But when an assassin's bullets shattered the dream, she showed the world that there was unimagined strength beneath the silk."

—Hugh Sidey, *Life* magazine

Although Jackie was by nature a fearless, independent person, few people imagined that there was such "strength beneath the silk." She was able to successfully call upon this trait during the awful days following the assassination of her husband. It was her strength, day after day, that offered a grieving nation hope that the future still mattered. Forever after, the word *courageous* has been the adjective used most often to describe Jackie Kennedy.

Many people, however, are unaware of the courage Jackie displayed immediately following the fatal shots fired in Dallas.

According to reporter Martha Duffy, "She was at her best in the crunch. When disaster struck in Dallas on Nov. 22, 1963, those who saw her said she was tearless, perhaps spacey, 'with a 50-yard stare.' But she knew what she had to do to fulfill her commitment to her husband, her children and her country. Her bright pink suit was soiled with blood and gray matter, but she would not change it or leave John F. Kennedy's body." When the limousine reached Parkland Hospital, Jackie was still holding her husband's head in her lap, literally trying to push his shattered brain back into his skull. It was only when one of Jack's aides put a jacket over the President's head did she allow him to be taken from her. When hospital physicians tried to keep her out of the trauma room, she forced her way past a nurse, refusing to be separated from Jack. When the casket arrived, the doctor tried to persuade Jackie to leave the room. "Do you think seeing the coffin can upset me, Doctor? I've seen my husband die, shot in my arms. His blood is all over me. How can I see anything worse than I've seen?"

Streak of Bravery from Birth

Although nothing in her life would match the horror of her husband's murder, Jackie's courage should not have surprised people, because she had always shown a streak of bravery and independent thinking. As a fresh-faced two-year-old, little Jackie was placed on a huge, brown horse and, much to the amazement of outsiders, she did not cry to get off but kept her grip. A few years later, she emerged as a full-fledged equestrienne. Another show of courage came when, as a four-year-old, Jackie was lost in New York's Central Park, having wandered away from her sister and nursemaid, as nannies were called then. Instead of breaking down in tears as most toddlers would have, she waited until she found a policeman and said, "My nurse is lost." Jackie gave the officer her phone number and he called her mother, who picked her up at the station house.

Jackie was eleven years old when her parents' marriage dissolved. Divorce in the 1940s was viewed as scandalous, and Jackie and her sister, Lee, were subjected to the cruel taunts and teases of other children whose parents undoubtedly gossiped about the breakup of the so-called glamorous marriage of Janet and Jack Bouvier. It was as if their family was at the top of the heap one day and at the bottom the next. Jackie bravely ignored these insults and developed a protective veil that few, if any, were allowed to penetrate. She quickly learned that the promise of love and security that marriage and family should provide could be destroyed in one fell swoop. Like the stately swan that glides gracefully through a storm while paddling ferociously beneath the water to keep up, Jackie learned to coolly confront a crisis, relying on her inner strength to get through her darkest days.

When one is alone and there's no one to provide encouragement or approval, it's even harder to be courageous. Jackie, at age eighteen, took a bold step when her grandfather, John Vernou Bouvier Jr. ("Grampy Jack"), died. Immediately following her grandfather's death, there was an unfortunate family squabble over his will. As money, status, and privilege were very important to the surviving members of the Bouvier family, all were concerned about the amount of their inheritance. Later, Jackie would recall, "I was sitting beside my grandfather's coffin, looking at him as he lay in his dark blue suit with his hands folded. I had never seen death before and was ashamed that it made no more of an impression. . . . I was glad he couldn't see how his children behaved once he was dead."

She then described how a gardener arrived at the wake and presented the family with a small bunch of violets. One of Jackie's more condescending aunts grabbed the humble bouquet, rather rudely according to Jackie, and stuck them into a larger bunch of flowers. Jackie recognized in the gardener's simple gift a gesture of love that was missing from her relatives. When her aunt told everyone to leave the room for the closing of the coffin, Jackie "knelt on the bench beside the coffin and put the violets down inside, beneath my grandfather's elbow, where the people who came to close the coffin could not see them." This spontaneous act of defiance was Jackie's way of protesting her relatives' poor behavior.

A Happy and Sad Day

Jackie's strength of character emerged again on what should have been the happiest day of her life—her marriage to Jack

Kennedy on September 12, 1953. The carefully constructed plans for her wedding promised everything for which a bride could hope. The *Newport Daily News* described it as the "most brilliant wedding in many years." Jackie wore a gown made of fifty yards of ivory silk taffeta, and her ten bridesmaids wore dresses of pink silk faille and red satin. The day was sunny, the bride was beautiful, and the groom was handsome. Archbishop Cushing of Boston, who conducted the nuptial mass, even read a special blessing from Pope Pius XII.

However, in spite of her serene countenance, and unknown to the nearly nine hundred people who packed St. Mary's Church, Jackie was close to tears. Just minutes before the ceremony, Jackie learned that her beloved father, Jack Bouvier, would not be escorting her down the aisle. Apparently, he was thought to be too tipsy, and "Hughdie" Auchincloss, Jackie's stepfather, gave her away instead. She knew how much her father had looked forward to this moment and how hurt he had felt after being excluded from the many prenuptial parties that were given, including the rehearsal dinner the night before the wedding. Black Jack had begun drinking the morning of the wedding after being told by his former wife that he would not be allowed to attend the reception at Hammersmith Farm, the Auchincloss's lavish Rhode Island estate.

When the processional march began and all eyes turned toward her, Jackie steadied herself and, at least outwardly, gave no indication of what had happened. Once again, she summoned the strength to rise above the hurt she felt and to portray, instead, the serene, beautiful bride whom everyone expected to see.

Jack's Hurtful Behavior

For Jackie, the absence of her father was the final blow in a series of disappointments leading up to her wedding. Worst of all, Jack's behavior following the announcement of their engagement hurt her deeply. Shortly after the news was released, Jack chartered a yacht in the south of France and headed there for a few weeks with several of his male friends, leaving Jackie back at Newport. Then, just before the wedding, he took Jackie aside and confessed that he was a hopeless womanizer. "Jack unloaded," Florida senator George Smathers said. "He confessed everything to Jackie. She handled it pretty well. She was aware that Jack was a Kennedy and that Joe [his father] had never been an example of virtue. Jack wasn't a surprise to her. Women of that class and generation were raised to turn a blind eye to sexual peccadilloes. But Jack talked too much, and he lived to regret that conversation. He was just like Jackie's father, Black Jack. Neither of those guys could change."

Even before Jack's confession, Jackie began to have serious reservations about his ability to remain faithful to her. She was very drawn to Jack and appeared to have thought that the love she felt for him could overcome any character flaw, just as most women in love have thought throughout the ages. Overlooking his behavior, she rationalized it was something most men do, including the father she so obviously loved and admired. On the day of her wedding reception, she spotted a family friend, Polly Tunney, who was the grandniece of Andrew Carnegie. Polly had shocked her WASP relatives when she married boxer Gene Tunney. Jackie took her aside and asked, "How does a married woman cope with an unfaithful husband?" Polly Tunney, amazed by the question, answered, "Well, my dear, I always believed in my heart that I was the one he loved." Certainly Jackie, as a new and hopeful bride, must have felt the same way, believing that she came first with Jack. In spite of his infidelity, Jackie loved her husband and was certain he felt the same way about her.

Jackie's decision to stay with Jack and her refusal to become a victim was an act of bravery that wouldn't have been possible had she been a weaker woman. Imperfect as it seemed, their marriage worked on so many different levels that neither Jackie nor Jack would ever have seriously considered ending it. Both experienced true joy in their life together, and Jackie, in spite of the hurt Jack's infidelity created, never excluded him from her heart, nor did he exclude her from his.

Some may disagree that it was courage that kept Jackie in her marriage. Many women today, especially those who are financially independent, might hesitate to stay in such a relationship. Because Jackie believed in Jack's essential goodness, she remained hopeful that he would change. Hope is a complex matter, a form of courage requiring a deliberate act of will to believe things can improve, that wrongs will right themselves. It was not in Jackie's makeup to give up, as she most probably viewed it as cowardly.

Jackie's strong will was evident from the beginning of Jack's presidency. As the new First Lady, she was determined to carve out her role as she saw fit, regardless of any potential criticism. With characteristic fortitude, she decided, not her staff, when it was appropriate to speak to the press. She also refused to be pressured to make her children available to the media, demanding privacy for them instead. She was not afraid to tackle projects others would have avoided, such as the formidable White House restoration.

During the Cuban Missile Crisis in the fall of 1962, Jackie's courage under fire was especially laudable. Many historians view that period as the finest moment of the Kennedy presidency. It was then that Jack Kennedy stared down the Soviet Union in the face of a possible nuclear attack on the United States. It was also a time when Jackie, too, would be severely tested.

During this time, Jackie projected an outward calm as she went about her duties as First Lady. In private, sensing the terrible burden her husband was under, she sought to lift his spirits by talking about what the children were up to, other family interests, and idle gossip. At one point, Jack told Jackie that it would be wise for her and the children to take refuge in a secret underground shelter just outside the capital. She refused to leave him alone in the White House and stayed there with their children.

When the crisis was over, President Kennedy presented his key advisors with silver replicas of a calendar with the thirteen days in October highlighted in recognition of their strength and courage during that difficult period. He also presented one to Jackie.

Ironically, in what turned out to be the final months of Jack Kennedy's life, the miracle that Jackie had hoped for seemed to occur. Jack changed his behavior. Following the death of their infant son, Patrick, who lived less than forty hours after his birth on August 7, 1963, Jack Kennedy's suppressed emotions came forth. For the first time that anyone could remember, he openly sobbed in front of close friends shortly after hearing that his son had died. Much to their amazement, friends also saw a new tenderness in Jackie and Jack's marriage. Jack openly caressed his wife in public and put aside some of his administrative duties, spending as much time with her and the children as possible.

The Day the World Stood Still

Life changed forever for Jackie Kennedy on the day her husband was murdered by Lee Harvey Oswald. Her courage before the world in handling Jack Kennedy's funeral will never be forgotten. At this point, America was supercharged with fear. For the first time in modern history, not only was the President assassinated, but two days later his reputed killer was shot down in cold blood as millions of television viewers watched. Hysteria and conspiracy theories ran rampant. Vice President Lyndon Baines Johnson, sworn in as the thirty-sixth president of the United States less than ninety-eight minutes after Kennedy was pronounced dead, was also thought to be a potential target.

In spite of those chilling circumstances, Jackie made the decision to walk in the funeral procession behind her husband's coffin, breaking the tradition for wives to follow by automobile. The White House security force was completely unnerved, as another assassin's bullet could possibly be unleashed. Jackie's brothers-in-law, Bobby and Teddy Kennedy, flanked her as they walked the eight blocks from the White House to St. Matthew's Cathedral. President Johnson, against the wishes of his advisers, also joined the march. More than forty leaders from around the world walked with the brave, thirty-four-year-old widow. Among them were France's General de Gaulle, Emperor Haile Selassie of Ethiopia, Britain's Prince Philip, and Soviet Foreign Minister Anastas Mikoyan.

Jackie touched all our hearts as she carried herself with dignity and courage—first at the Capitol Rotunda, then along the route of the funeral procession, and during the sad days and weeks that followed.

Jackie had never been so alone in her life. Gone was the husband who had meant everything to her. She had lost her life's purpose and, in the process, was also forced to abruptly leave the White House, the home where she and Jack had shared so many magnificent moments together during their three years as President and First Lady. With Lyndon Johnson's assumption of the presidency immediately following the assassination, he and his family would now occupy the executive mansion Jackie had so painstakingly restored.

A Move to New York

What courage it must have taken Jackie every day to wake up, put one foot in front of the other, and try to preserve a semblance of normalcy for her children. After a brief residency in a house in Georgetown, Jackie decided to move to New York, a city she had lived in and loved as a child, as it offered more anonymity. Now that Jack was gone, Washington held little for her except the awful knowledge that because of his presidency her husband had been taken from her.

In 1964, Jackie purchased an apartment at 1040 Fifth Avenue on the upper east side of Manhattan. At first, she closeted herself at home, refusing to meet with anyone and wanting to be alone with her sorrow. She felt her first duty was to her children, Caroline and John, and she reserved all her strength for them. Eventually she emerged from her self-imposed solitude and began seeing friends and prospective suitors. She thought she had found one in the person of Aristotle Onassis, and they married in 1968.

Jackie as Working Woman

The marriage turned out to be far from happy for both of them, and they were in the process of getting a divorce when Onassis died in 1975. A widow once again, Jackie floundered for a while until a friend suggested she return to work. As Jackie lived in a celebrity fishbowl, with her every action constantly scrutinized, she must have carefully deliberated the consequences of returning to the workplace after an absence of more than twenty-two years. In the fall of 1975, Jackie took a job in publishing, realizing the world would be watching to see if she failed. This didn't seem likely, because Jackie, an excellent writer and editor, was well suited to her job.

One of her first projects was a rather bland book titled *Remember the Ladies*, which focused on American women between 1750 and 1815. It was not exactly a huge success, but as Jackie grew to get a better feel for the book business, she moved on to more substantial fare.

As an editor with a high profile and a passionate devotion to the arts, Jackie was able to seek out celebrities and artists and persuade them to write about their worlds. When Gelsey Kirkland, the celebrated ballerina of the New York City

Ballet, agreed to write her life story, Jackie discovered that Kirkland's revelations about her drug-fueled, anorexic life—including her use of amphetamines supplied by company founder George Balanchine—would be controversial and possibly damaging to the ballet community. *Publishers Weekly*'s review (1986) acknowledged the memoir served "as a devastating critique of the American dance establishment that cannot be ignored." It was a mark of Jackie's professional courage that she championed *Dancing on My Grave* to its ultimate success as her first best-seller.

The Final Battle

She continued to be as active as ever and even told Charles Whitehouse, a riding companion, that she never felt tired after a vigorous ride on horseback because her jogs around Central Park kept her fit. In November 1993, Jackie unexpectedly fell off her horse. A medical examination revealed a swollen lymph node in her groin. Thinking it was a sign of infection, she was treated with antibiotics. However, Jackie began to feel increasingly weak and was forced to cancel some of her activities, including various editorial meetings at Doubleday. Outwardly her spirits were as bright as ever, and she eagerly looked forward to the holiday season with her family and her close companion, Maurice Tempelsman.

After Christmas, Jackie and Maurice went on a Caribbean

cruise and suddenly she became ill, suffering sharp pains in her back and abdomen. Doctors detected a second swollen lymph node in her neck. She was given a battery of tests at New York Hospital Cornell Medical Center to determine the nature of her illness. When the reports came in, Jackie learned she had non-Hodgkin's lymphoma, a virulent form of cancer that is known to spread quickly throughout the body. Reacting with characteristic calmness, she was determined to overcome yet another obstacle thrown into her life's path.

Her courage was such that she told friends her cancer was simply an annoyance and that soon everything would be all right. She infused those around her with hope and still managed to carry on her life, although increasingly diminished at this point. She underwent aggressive chemotherapy treatments, eventually losing her hair and forced to wear a wig. Yet she still came to the office insisting that the medical procedures were not that bad, as they allowed her time to read when the drugs were being pumped into her arm.

Jackie battled cancer quietly and courageously until she realized there was no hope that she could successfully win. Characteristically, she did it her way, asking that all treatment be discontinued and that she be taken home. She died on Thursday, May 19, 1994, at 10:15 p.m. Her son, John Kennedy Jr., said to reporters that his mother died "surrounded by her friends and her family and her books and the people and the things that she loved. And she did it in her own way and on her own terms." Even after so many years since her death, Jackie's life continues to demonstrate that it takes strength and courage to hold on to our centers during times of great hurt. She met each crisis not only with courage but also with a total lack of self-pity; whether it was the loss of a loved one, betrayal, or her own impending death. Jackie was never a victim. She didn't wallow in despair but forced herself to look forward in hope. She accepted both her life and death in the same spirit—with courage and the knowledge that life must go on until the final curtain is drawn.

Newspapers, magazines, and television news reports ran long and sympathetic stories about her life and death. Perhaps the most succinct and tender one was the headline in the *New York Daily News*—"Missing Her."

What Jackie Taught Us

There is no doubt that courage, one of the noblest elements of the human soul, was a dominant current that ran through the life of Jacqueline Kennedy Onassis. Her life demonstrates that courage begins with taking the small steps that challenge us, and that the more often we're courageous, the more courageous we become.

Most of us would like to think of ourselves as courageous. However, until we're faced with danger, failure, or opposition, it's impossible to know if we are or aren't. Courage can mean taking a stand that sets you apart from your family or friends. Courage is doing what you say you will no matter how great the cost. Courage can be living up to your vows or principles even when those around you are not.

Jackie taught us that possessing courage is pivotal to surviving life's most awful moments. Her bravery inspires us to make a conscious effort to confront our daily setbacks with poise, dignity, and the determination to get on with our lives.

Throughout her life, Jackie faced many circumstances that might well have broken the spirit of someone with lesser strength. Although she suffered depression and sometimes despair, particularly after her husband's assassination, she eventually emerged whole, even stronger than before. Therein lies the essence of courage: the ability to withstand the most painful moments without crumbling.

Courage is a quiet virtue and often arrives unannounced. We may not even realize it when we are acting courageously, but it doesn't matter. Once courageous, always courageous. If we can look fear in the face and refuse to be cowed, our strength will emerge. We can each become more courageous by believing that we can be.

It's equally important for each of us to remember that courage can be contagious and, invariably, the world is made a better place because of it.

The Lion and the Lioness

Allen Packwood is the director of the Churchill Archives
Centre at the University of Cambridge, England.

with Tina Santi Flaherty

*I*N THE DARK days and darker nights when Britain stood
alone—and most men save Englishmen despaired of
England's life—he mobilized the English language and sent it
into battle. The incandescent quality of his words illuminated
the courage of his countrymen."

It was with these words, on April 9, 1963, that President
John F. Kennedy conferred the award of Honorary United
States Citizenship to Sir Winston Churchill, a rare and high
honor to this day, and the first of its kind to be bestowed by an
act of Congress. Sir Winston was too old and too frail to cross
the Atlantic to receive the award in person, but he was represented by his son, Randolph, and by his grandson and name-
sake, Winston Churchill. The First Lady was present to

witness the historic ceremony, a cheerful spring event in the White House Rose Garden that celebrated human courage. Little could she know then that the greatest test of her own character and courage lay just a few months in the future.

Churchill's career illustrates that there are many expressions of bravery. When he was only twenty-one, he came under fire for the first time in Cuba during the Spanish conflict. He actively sought adventure thereafter in India, the Sudan, and South Africa. He had charged with the Twenty-First Lancers at the Battle of Omdurman and had escaped from a Boer prison. Throughout his life he was drawn to physical danger: learning to fly in primitive airplanes, serving a spell in the trenches of World War I, walking the streets of London during the Blitz, and undertaking dangerous journeys across U-boat-infested waters.

But the older Churchill represents a different kind of courage. He often found himself on the wrong side of many debates and heavily criticized for some of his views. He had not always been right. Yet in the 1930s he saw far more clearly than most the dangers of a disarmed Britain and a revived militaristic Nazi Germany. He had become the most vocal and high-profile critic of Prime Minister Chamberlain's appeasement policy. Above all, he had shown the moral courage and the self-belief to assume the leadership of his country and to identify himself with the fight against Hitler. Churchill of course famously and modestly declared that it was the British people who had been the lion, and it had simply fallen upon him to give the lion's roar. The truth was that it took great bravery to give that roar.

If Churchill was a lion, then Jacqueline Kennedy was a lioness. Like Churchill she also chose the public path, marrying into a life of sacrifice and duty. Like Churchill's stand in 1940, her own dignified walk with destiny at the state funeral of her husband struck a chord in the national psyche of America, and for that moment she too became a symbol of human and moral courage. And like the lioness she worked tirelessly to defend her husband's reputation in death as in life.

In the years following the assassination, Jackie fiercely protected the safety and privacy of her children so that she could do the job that mattered most. "If you bungle raising your children," she said, "I don't think whatever else you do matters very much." As Ted Kennedy said about Caroline and John Jr., they are her "two miracles."

Jackie was always known for the courage of her convictions. Her refusal to bend to public opinion is one of her defining characteristics. When she married Aristotle Onassis in 1968, she ignored critics who said she would alienate her admiring public. After the assassination of her brother-in-law Senator Robert F. Kennedy four months earlier, she was particularly concerned for the safety of her children, as she came to believe that all Kennedys were targets for murder. With an estate on a private island

and an army of seventy-five, the wealthy Onassis offered a protected world where she and her children could be safe.

After Onassis's death in 1975, Jackie's iconoclasm continued. She took a job in publishing, which removed her from the limelight. It was a brave decision, as the world was watching to see if she would fail or succeed in her role as a workingwoman. In praising her abilities, Stephen Rubin, then president and publisher of Doubleday where she was employed, said, "Few people understood how committed and talented she was at the work she chose to do."

When Jackie learned she had non-Hodgkin's lymphoma in 1993, a viral form of cancer, she faced it with a kind of calmness that few people could muster. Her courage was such that she insisted on living her life as she always did, telling friends that soon everything would be all right. She even said chemotherapy was not that bad as it gave her a chance to read a good book. In announcing her death, her son, John F. Kennedy Jr., stated that she'd died as she lived: "in her own way and on her terms. And we all feel lucky for that."

"Courage is rightly esteemed the first of human qualities because, as has been said, it is the quality which guarantees all others." Winston Churchill wrote these words about King Alfonso XIII of Spain, a ruler who survived a violent assassination attempt in 1906. They would seem to apply equally well to Jacqueline Kennedy Onassis.

"More than any other woman of her time, she captivated our nation and the world with her intelligence, her elegance, and her grace. Even in the face of impossible tragedy, she carried the grief of her family and our entire nation with a calm power that somehow reassured all the rest of us."

—BILL CLINTON

What Jackie Taught Us About

Focus

"She [Jackie] was determined, self-disciplined, with a sense of clear purpose that she carried out with a desire for perfection. Her capacity for concentration, whether it be exhibited in amusing storytelling, both real and imaginative, her thought-ful writing, her whimsical drawing, was finely focused."
—Yusha Auchincloss, Jackie's stepbrother

*A*LWAYS IN TUNE with the times, Jackie was a modern woman whose approach to life personified the changing role of women in America during the second half of the twen-tieth century. Extremely disciplined, she had enormous powers of concentration that enabled her to accomplish virtually any-thing she set out to do. Like most successful individuals, she avoided distractions and never lost sight of the big picture.

Even as a young girl, Jackie was focused on accomplishing

her goals. She had a passion to excel in whatever she did, finding it impossible to settle for less. Her mother, Janet Bouvier, was intensely competitive and undoubtedly passed on this trait to Jackie. As a child of five, Jackie was photographed leading her pony away from the ring, visibly angry at losing a competition. Her mother, trapped in an unhappy marriage to John "Jack" V. Bouvier III, was a perfectionist, and pushed both her daughters to achieve. She was extremely critical when they failed to live up to her high standards. Although Jackie loved her father more, her life was driven by her need to please her mother.

As a nineteen-year-old college student at Vassar, Jackie announced that as soon as she completed her sophomore year, she intended to study abroad at the Sorbonne in Paris. An eye-opening trip to Europe between her freshman and sophomore years had convinced Jackie that studying in a foreign country could teach her far more than spending the time in the isolated environs of Vassar, located in Poughkeepsie, a small town about two hours away from New York City.

For Jackie to leave Vassar was unthinkable to her father and mother, now divorced and remarried to a wealthy stockbroker, Hugh ("Hughdie") D. Auchincloss Jr. It was especially difficult for Jackie to go against the wishes of her father, who doted on her. With his reduced living circumstances and excessive drinking, "Black Jack" Bouvier had become even more emotionally dependent on his daughter, and it was readily apparent how much he wanted her to stay in New York. Her mother, Janet, however, was more concerned that somehow Jackie would be seduced by the lively bohemian culture of France and become estranged from the orderly Auchincloss world of wealth and privilege, perhaps never to return to the United States. Also, neither Janet nor Hughdie, Jackie's stepfather, welcomed the prospect of additional expenses that the undertaking would entail.

Although faced with a rare, united front of opposition from both her parents, Jackie refused to be discouraged. Studying abroad was not a whimsical wish in her mind; this was something that really mattered to her. Jackie felt she had earned the courage of her convictions, as she had treated her trip to Europe the previous summer as an opportunity to learn, not just to sightsee. Prior to leaving for Europe, she read history books and studied French, German, and Italian in order to be fully prepared to gain as much knowledge as possible. She was determined to return to the continent and would not be discouraged.

Jackie even went so far as to threaten that she would move to New York City and become a model if her parents wouldn't let her go. Reluctantly, they did. This act of defiance by a young female, with little experience in life, was not generally acceptable behavior at the time. Jackie's determination, however, was stronger than any words her parents could say, and she intended to follow the path that felt right to her. This was an attitude that she displayed for the rest of her life.

The Rules According to Jackie

Jackie was able to stay focused on her priorities by saying "no" to any distraction that confronted her—something not everyone can or will do. It was reason enough for her to decline an activity if she found it unnecessary, boring, or a waste of her time—a trait she probably inherited from her father, who was notoriously intolerant of bores. Undoubtedly, Jackie realized that if she ever was to achieve what really made her happy, she had to set standards and hold fast to them.

Jackie did capitulate when she believed it was absolutely necessary—a serious request from her husband, for example—but she set limits before she would agree to do something. When Jack Kennedy first asked her to help him campaign for his presidential run, she initially rejected the idea. Later, she became involved, but only in those areas she thought important. She applied the same discipline when it came to handling the media, advising her press staff, "My press relations will be minimum information given with maximum politeness..." Wasn't speaking to the press part of her job as First Lady? Yes, but again, Jackie taught us that we could take charge of our lives and decide for ourselves what our role will be.

In any endeavor that reflected on her ability as the wife of the President, she rarely delegated anything except the least important matters. Scrupulously organized, Jackie was never without a stack of yellow memo pads by her bed. Whenever she thought of something she would jot it down on her to-do list, even in the middle of the night. This habit proved very useful in her restoration of the 132 rooms of the White House. She personally examined more than twenty-five thousand artifacts located in the mansion's storage space before she decided what belonged or didn't.

Refusal to Accept Defeat

Jackie orchestrated the elegant state dinners as a director would an opening night performance, leaving no detail to chance lest it take away from the overall effect. The dinner she planned for Pakistan's President Ayub Khan at Mount Vernon, the home of George Washington, in July 1961, was a triumph of her indomitable will against overwhelming odds. For practical reasons, state dinners had never been held outside the White House, and Jackie's decision to do otherwise presented serious organizational challenges. So complex were the logistics of the event that one of the military aides compared it to the complicated preparations for a full-scale battle.

Inspired by the celebratory dinner General de Gaulle held in the Kennedys' honor at Versailles during their trip to Paris a few months earlier, Jackie wanted the evening at Mount Vernon to re-create America's historic beginnings. When she initially unleashed her ambitious plan to host a state dinner there, she gave her staff a four-week deadline. They were quick to list the seemingly insurmountable problems: no electricity or refrigeration, a crude kitchen, minimal bathroom facilities, and the annoyance of mosquitoes.

"As those around her doubted that we could pull it off, Jackie remained serene and confident in her staff's abilities," recalled Tish Baldrige. "Her innate control of endless details and superb sense of organization were accompanied by a quiet little phrase of iron, 'Of course it can be done.'"

The food was cooked at the White House and transported by truck to Mount Vernon along with tables, chairs, linens, china, crystal, and even generators. The guests traveled via boat along the Potomac, arriving to see a reenactment of a Revolutionary War drill. They were served dinner in a green tent with a butter yellow lining decorated by Tiffany's and then heard the National Symphony Orchestra. It was theater at its best. Jackie had achieved what seemed impossible a few short weeks earlier.

That Jackie Kennedy did not easily take no for an answer is an understatement. In fact, she was known to have little tolerance for losing and would go to great lengths to outfox people who tried to deny her. Like most high achievers, Jackie—when faced with an obstacle—either pushed through the roadblock or found a way around it. She did not cave.

When James Biddle, a curator at the Metropolitan Museum of Art, refused to lend the White House an important silver centerpiece, Jackie dug in her heels. She asked again, but Biddle would not budge. Unwilling to be denied and determined to get what she wanted, Jackie waited until he went on vacation and retrieved the centerpiece. Wanting him to realize that he had made a serious error in judgment, she sent Biddle a handwritten note, which he found on his desk when he returned from holiday: "Darling Jimmy, I've got it. . . . Jacqueline Kennedy, The White House."

Jackie's desire that all furnishings in the soon-to-be restored White House be authentically accurate led to another ingenious display of her tenacious mind-set. She was determined to retrieve a crystal chandelier that originally belonged to the White House and was now hanging in the Capitol. Although it had been sold during the Theodore Roosevelt administration, Jackie thought it would be perfect for the newly restored rooms. She asked David Finley, a member of the White House Historical Association, to approach George Steward, architect of the Capitol, and ask for the chandelier's return.

Surprisingly, Steward turned down Jackie and added that it might require an act of Congress to transfer such an item to the White House. He further irritated her by stating that the three crystal chandeliers that originally hung in the executive mansion "do not conform to the period of the restored White House." To be so bluntly rebuffed and then lectured as to what was appropriate for the White House was unacceptable to

Jackie. She tried a new tactic, this time imploring "dear" Lyndon Johnson, the vice president, in a six-page handwritten letter to help her. Johnson, who was ever charmed by Jackie, tried to persuade Steward to go along with Jackie's request. Steward stood his ground and told Johnson that it was impossible.

Now it was all-out war in Jackie's mind. That someone should try to thwart her in a matter that she felt so passionate about inspired her to even greater heights to get what she wanted. She pulled out her trump card, writing Steward that the chandelier in question was to be hung in the newly restored Treaty Room, which was soon to be unveiled for the press. If he did not give it to her, she not-so-subtly threatened, she would be forced to go to the newspapers and reveal how Steward refused to cooperate. She turned to Johnson again, suggesting that he tell Steward that she needed the chandelier for only one day when the press was to be invited. She also told Johnson that she would find a way to keep it permanently. Ten days later, she got her chandelier.

A Clear Sense of Purpose

During the aftermath of her husband's assassination in Dallas and his subsequent funeral and burial, Jackie brought all her powers of concentration to bear. Winston Churchill, one of John Kennedy's greatest heroes, could have been describing her attitude when he urged, "If you are going through hell, keep going." Despite her tremendous pain and deep emotional anguish, Jackie scrutinized history books that described in detail the funerals of the world's great leaders. Utilizing this information, she planned every aspect of her husband's final farewell to ensure that it accurately reflected his legacy as she saw it.

It was Jackie who asked for the riderless horse—a never-to-be-forgotten symbol of Abraham Lincoln's funeral—and it was Jackie who arranged for the haunting Irish bagpipe music that Jack loved so much. It also was Jackie who proposed the idea of the Eternal Flame to be placed beside her husband's grave at Arlington National Cemetery, and it was she who chose the simple daisies, white chrysanthemums, and stephanotis for the altar vases at his funeral mass. Jackie also made sure that their three-year-old son, John Jr., saluted his father's coffin as it passed by in the funeral procession.

Even though she was emotionally drained, Jackie insisted on going through with a birthday party that had already been planned for her son John on the same day as the funeral.

Immediately after the assassination, she uncharacteristically gave interviews to writers and journalists with the intention of setting the tone of her husband's presidency for the history books. In the weeks, months, and years that followed, she single-mindedly went about what she believed was now her life's purpose—to keep alive the glory of her husband's presidency.

In early 1964, Jackie learned that several books about the

assassination were already under way and tried unsuccessfully to dissuade the authors from continuing their projects. So intent was she on preserving Jack's legacy as she saw it that she decided to personally select an author who would write an account to her liking. After two writers declined, including Theodore White, she approached William Manchester, who had previously written a positive book about Jack. Manchester was certain that he was chosen because "she thought I would be manageable." After all, he had submitted his prior book to Jack to review before publication.

Manchester agreed to an arrangement that gave the Kennedys approval of the final draft—a decision that turned out to be a bad idea for all concerned. Over a period of months, beginning in April 1964, Jackie sat with Manchester for hours of tape-recorded interviews. Still in shock from the assassination, she shared many personal memories with him that she would live to regret. Manchester dutifully handed over copies of his 1,201-page manuscript to Jackie and her brother-in-law, Robert Kennedy, both of whom demanded countless revisions. While Manchester accepted many of the changes Jackie and Bobby requested, there were some he refused to make.

Although Manchester produced a credible book, Jackie was distraught over certain passages that she viewed as a violation of her privacy as well as that of her children. When she learned he had sold the serialization rights to *Look* magazine for $650,000—the largest magazine sale in history—she became outraged that he would commercialize the book in such a manner. She had envisioned a book that would be a historical account that would sit mostly on library shelves and be read by scholars, students, and researchers. She had not counted on Manchester's engaging style that bordered on the dramatic or having portions of the book published in one of the country's leading magazines. Meetings with Manchester and *Look* magazine executives were fruitless.

Although emotionally wrenched and bitterly disappointed, Jackie persisted. Finally, she decided to do the unthinkable. Shocking everyone, including Bobby, Jackie announced that she was filing suit against publishing house Harper & Row, *Look* magazine, and William Manchester to prevent publication of *Death of a President*.

The suit was settled within weeks, and Jackie won most of the changes that she wanted. However, she was vilified in front-page stories throughout the world. As biographer Sarah Bradford observed, "What she saw as a courageous defense of her rights in the face of betrayal of confidentiality, the American public perceived as an arrogant abuse of power and an attempt to stifle their cherished right of freedom and speech."

Her Thoughtful Writing

Jackie's life demonstrated how important focus is even in the everyday things of life. Her penchant for sending carefully thought-out letters is well known. She followed a rigid rule that all thank you notes should be written within twenty-four hours. These beautifully written missives were warm, charming, and personal, never stiff or dutiful, and one of the few avenues where Jackie felt free to reveal her feelings. She used the opportunity not only to communicate her appreciation but to convey how she felt about the person as well.

A touching example is the letter Jackie sent to President and Mrs. Nixon following her visit with John and Caroline to the White House on February 3, 1971, to view the newly unveiled portraits of John and Jacqueline Kennedy. It was Jackie's first visit to the White House since 1963, and she apparently was dreading it. The Nixons took measures to make her and the children as comfortable as possible, banning all press and arranging for a quiet, private dinner.

Afterward, using a dark blue pen on light blue stationery, Jackie wrote:

Dear Mr. President
Dear Mrs. Nixon.

You were so kind to us yesterday. Never have I seen such magnanimity and such tenderness.

Can you imagine the gift you gave me? To return to the White House privately with my little ones while they are still young enough to rediscover their childhood—with you both as guides—and with your daughters, such extraordinary young women.

What a tribute to have brought them up like that in the limelight. I pray I can do half the same with my Caroline. It was good to see her exposed to their example, and John to their charm!

You spoiled us beyond belief; the Jet Star, our tour, the superb dinner. Thank you, Mr. President, for opening one of your precious bottles of Bordeaux for us.

I have never seen the White House look so perfect. There is no hidden corner of it that is not beautiful now. It was moving, when we left, to see the great House illuminated, with the fountains playing.

The way you have hung the portraits does them great honor—more than they deserve. They should not have been such trouble to you. You bent over backwards to be generous, and we are all deeply touched and grateful.

It made me happy to hear the children bursting with reminiscences all the way home.

Before John went to sleep, I could explain the photographs of Jack and him in his room, to him. "There you are with Daddy right where the President was describing the Great Seal; there, on the path where the President accompanied us to our car."

Your kindness made real memories of his shadowy ones.
Thank you with all my heart. A day I always dreaded
turned out to be one of the most precious ones I have spent
with my children.
May God bless you all.

Most gratefully,
Jackie

(Courtesy, Richard Nixon Library and Birthplace)

Her letter is dated February 4. As was her habit, Jackie wrote her lovely note within a day of her visit.

Even at the bleakest point of her life, Jackie's discipline didn't waver. The day after her husband was buried, she took the time to write a lengthy letter of appreciation to Lyndon Johnson, thanking him for walking behind Jack's coffin despite the security risks and for his friendship over the years. She even apologized for any disturbance that the outdoor play of Caroline's White House nursery school might be causing and promised that they would soon be gone.

The status or importance of the person had no influence on Jackie's sense of propriety when it came to thank you notes. The sales staff at Bergdorf Goodman, an exclusive department store in New York City where she did much of her shopping, still treasures the personal notes they received from her.

Legendary Self-Discipline

Throughout her life, Jackie's self-discipline was legendary, and especially so when it came to her focus on maintaining a trim figure. This was a trait that she inherited from her handsome father, Jack Bouvier, who had a fine muscular physique and stayed in shape with daily workouts. One of the ways Jackie kept limber was with yoga, to which Prime Minister Nehru had introduced her in India in 1962. According to New Yorker Dale Coudert, who took classes with her in the early 1980s over a three-year period, "Jackie impressed me as being very serious about everything she did, including yoga. I wasn't surprised she was better at it than I was."

Tilly Weitzner, Jackie's long-time yoga instructor, was very impressed by her star pupil's ability to master the discipline. "She was an excellent student because she had 100% concentration. . . . I taught Jackie yoga for 17 years, up until a month before she died. She was totally focused on what we were trying to accomplish and achieved a high degree of flexibility over the years."

Unlike many of Weitzner's students, Jackie rarely interrupted her sessions to take phone calls. "I can remember only two exceptions," Weitzner recalled, "whenever her friend Maurice Tempelsman phoned and the time when Michael Jackson insisted on speaking to her."

She also was careful not to overeat. Her friend and social

secretary, Tish Baldrige, said, "She watched the scale with the rigor of a diamond merchant counting his carats." She drank only water and ate nothing but fruit following a day when she thought she had eaten too much. This dietary regimen may sound tough to follow, but it worked for Jackie. As a rule, she ate sparingly throughout her life. A colleague from her publishing days remembers lunching with Jackie in her office when she was "munching on celery and carrots that she'd brought from home in tin foil." Her favorite diet dinner was said to be a baked potato with caviar.

Laserlike Focus

Jackie earned a reputation for being highly disciplined, with a laserlike focus on the essential elements of any project she undertook. Some of her greatest achievements were a result of this ability. Ensuring Jack's legacy as president was now her primary mission in life. In short order, she successfully worked toward the establishment of the Kennedy Center for the Performing Arts, the Kennedy Space Center, and the John F. Kennedy Library. She routinely, and almost compulsively, set the highest and most exacting standards for herself. Her life teaches us that by keeping focused on what matters most to us, we're much more likely to finish farther than we ever thought possible.

What Jackie Taught Us

How often do we waste countless hours doing things we don't really care about just because someone else says it's important? Jackie's life teaches us that if we want to get something done, we have to learn to say no and focus on our priorities.

Jacqueline Kennedy Onassis spent her time doing those things that really mattered to her, while not appearing to feel the least bit guilty for refusing to do something she didn't want to. She was clear in her mind as to what her priorities were because she knew *who* she was and *what* she wanted to accomplish.

In a busy world where we're constantly bombarded by distractions, it can be difficult to maintain our sense of purpose. We're only human, and it's easy to find a thousand and one excuses for failing to stay on track. If we are to accomplish anything worthwhile in life, we have to be selfish in our dedication to doing so. Jackie's example teaches us that we must set standards and goals for ourselves and stand by them. This may mean refusing to do something someone insists we must, or even taking as simple an action as cutting off a long-winded telephone conversation. It's not necessary to put everyone else's needs before our own in order to be a good and decent person. Some people spend their lives trying to be useful, while others just are.

Follow-through is a natural outgrowth of focus. When Jackie said she was going to do something, she did it. How many of us promise to do a simple favor for a friend and then don't follow through? If we are to be considered responsible human beings, we are accountable for what we say we'll do.

Whenever Jackie wanted to accomplish something, whether it was the restoration of the White House, establishing a play school for Caroline, or editing a book, she refused to let anyone or anything pull her away from any job she considered important. An optimistic person by nature, Jackie believed that whatever she wanted to accomplish could be done if she put her mind to it. It's our job to recognize that optimism, unlike pessimism, keeps our minds open to opportunities. When we are negative and believe something is beyond our reach, we often overlook the solution because we're concentrating too much on the problem. Jackie's life teaches us that when we act as if it is impossible to fail, we probably won't.

Jackie . . . with a Clear Sense of Purpose

Kent Barwick is president emeritus of the
Municipal Art Society.

*"Her innate control of endless details and superb sense of
organization were accompanied by a quiet little phrase of
iron, 'Of course it can be done.'"*

—LETITIA BALDRIGE

AFTER THE TRAGIC events of 1963 the former First Lady
left Washington and returned with her young children
to a new and presumably quieter life in New York. Despite
New York's deserved reputation as a frenetic center of activity,
the city can also be a good place to cherish the absence of public
attention. There's a long tradition of prominent people taking
refuge in New York, where anonymity is a basic civil right and
local custom grants film stars, tycoons, and deposed heads of

state the courtesy of pretending not to notice they are in our midst.

Occasionally one catches glimpses of our hidden celebrities in the Style section of the *Times*, and every so often after Jackie moved to New York a photograph would appear showing her stepping out of a car in front of Lincoln Center or the Metropolitan Museum beautifully dressed and elegantly remote. There was no hint that she would decide to step into the streets of the city and get involved as a citizen advocate in the often rough-and-tumble fights over development in New York.

It started in 1975. After reading a front-page newspaper story on a court decision that might doom New York's beloved Grand Central Terminal, Jackie telephoned the Municipal Art Society, where I was then working as executive director. We had just announced (somewhat whistling in the dark) that we were starting a campaign to save the terminal. She was direct: "I want to help." I was astonished that Jackie Kennedy Onassis was calling but went on to tell her, "Well, we're hoping to have a press conference to announce that we're forming the Committee to Save Grand Central, I'll be sure to give you plenty of notice."

She said, "I'm sure I can make it, just let me know."

I continued, deferentially, "We are drafting a public statement, and I'll send it over to your staff."

She said, "I don't have a staff, just send it to me."

True to her word she read, edited, and improved the statement and showed up a few days later at the press conference. Several prominent people spoke eloquently and at some length, but when her turn came she summed up with a short sentence delivered in a soft voice what the struggle was about. "If we don't care about our past, we cannot hope for the future." In this way, Grand Central was placed in front of the nation like the White House she had restored a decade earlier as a symbol of our national character.

The fight announced that day would drag on through the courts for years, but Jackie's words resonated with the country. The Committee to Save Grand Central received small donations with handwritten notes from people all across America. Other major cities joined the case as amici curiae, understanding that the ability of every American community to preserve its past and shape its future was at stake.

In the struggle for Grand Central, Jackie proved to be as effective a strategist backstage as she was as a spokeswoman in front of the cameras. She worried the fight would be over before it began if the city of New York didn't quickly appeal the lower court's decision. She sat down and wrote in longhand a personal letter to the incoming mayor, Abe Beame, knowing that his aides had recommended dropping the case. The letter began, "Dear Abe, President Kennedy so loved Grand Central . . ." It's possible without this personal touch the glorious facade and sculpture of Grand Central would be buried today in the Jersey Meadows alongside the broken columns of the demolished Pennsylvania Station. Happily, the city decided to fight.

The process of preparing legal briefs and arguing in front of various appeals courts was painstakingly slow and invisible to the public. Jackie and her colleagues at MAS, like Fred Papert, the advertising guru, knew the issue had to be kept alive and in front of the public.

Taking a leaf from the successful political campaigns organized by the Kennedys, the committee decided to go on the offensive. There were rallies and noontime concerts with Broadway stars. A storefront was set up in the adjacent Biltmore Hotel with T-shirts for the youth, neckties for the older crowd, and even bumper stickers for commuters to take home to the suburbs. J. Walter Thompson, a leading advertising agency, placed stories in newspapers around the country on a regular basis.

As the case reached the ultimate point of decision, the U.S. Supreme Court, the MAS organized a special train to carry cultural leaders, politicians, and prominent citizens to Washington. The "Landmark Express" was given a great send-off press conference with New York's new mayor, Ed Koch, along with other elected officials. When the train arrived at Washington's Union Station a huge crowd led by Senator Pat Moynihan and Joan Mondale, the vice president's wife, greeted Jackie and the committee with signs and cheers.

The Supreme Court's decision to affirm the constitutionality of New York's Landmarks Law was a great victory for the city's legal department and the Municipal Art Society's distinguished team of volunteer attorneys from prominent firms who had supported the city every step of the way. However the public's understanding of what this decision meant, the idea that it was legitimate for Americans to preserve history and great works of architecture, was clearly the product of Jackie's instincts and journalistic discipline to keep the focus on the essence of the issue.

These same abilities made her an invaluable leader of other MAS initiatives to protect the livability of New York. When the city government was about to approve (and share in the profits from) an outsize building at Columbus Circle so tall that it would have cast a mile-long shadow over Central Park, Jackie immediately observed, "They're stealing our sky." Her statement crystallized the issue, and what could have been an obscure and incomprehensible debate among lawyers and bureaucrats became an elementary public issue, the right of city dwellers to air and sunlight. The proposal was ultimately defeated.

When the city government stood by as the once-grand theaters and movie houses of Broadway and Forty-Second Street declined into an unsavory district of crime and pornography, Jackie and the MAS pitched in, under the leadership of Fred Papert, to create a vision of what the area could be with new entertainment uses, new restaurants, and new transportation. Others followed their lead and today the theaters are restored, the massage parlors are gone, replaced by new lively off-Broadway venues and cafés, and Times Square is one of the world's most popular tourist locations.

Jackie's self-discipline and strong focus were exhibited dramatically when the MAS took up a statewide issue. There had been a much publicized fight in the city when St. Bartholomew's Episcopal Church on Park Avenue wanted to put a fifty-nine-story office tower on top of their community house, a designated landmark. The Landmarks Commission denied permission. Spurning the offer of leading citizens, including Jackie and Brooke Astor, to help raise money to meet their needs, St. Bart's went to court instead and lost at every level. After the case was lost, a number of church groups joined forces with the purpose of persuading the legislature in Albany to pass the Flynn-Walsh bill, which would exempt all religious buildings in New York State from preservation laws. Hearings were held on the bill in cities throughout the state. The vast majority of the citizens who testified opposed the idea of the state interfering with local laws protecting landmarks, but the leaders in Albany seemed determined to pass the bill.

There would be a final and presumably perfunctory hearing in Albany before the vote. Once again MAS decided to create a "Landmark Express" train, which would carry Jackie and other preservation supporters from New York City picking up allies at each stop along the Hudson River route to Albany. The special train left early in the morning for what proved to be a grueling day. First there were meetings with Governor Mario Cuomo and the heads of the state senate and assembly. As we walked from meeting to meeting along the vast corridors in the capitol, state workers gathered to wave to Jackie. She waved back. Then there was a press conference with many advocates from around the state speaking on why the bill was wrong. Finally (or, so we thought) there was the hearing itself. Jackie testified, saying how important it was to preserve the truly outstanding churches of our state.

As the hearing concluded, it was getting to late afternoon and time to get back on the train home. But as we filed out of the room the chair of the hearing (who was also the sponsor of the Flynn-Walsh bill) asked if Jackie wouldn't mind having her picture taken with "a few" of the legislators. She agreed, and a camera was quickly set up in an adjacent conference room. Then, one by one, legislators began to appear. A line formed. Each would stand next to Jackie and then smile as the shutter clicked. There were many smiles and many clicks. My recollection is that this went on for over an hour and a half. Jackie, like all of us, must have been starved and thirsty and sore from standing all day without a break, but she knew why she was there and carried on. Jackie's relentless hard work, focus, and stamina were remarkable, and they were effective. The legislators, presumably busy with framing their new photographs, dropped the bill.

Jackie will always be remembered for saving Grand Central. But the enduring even greater gift to the country was her willingness to stand up for what she believed, even if it meant confronting those in power. When Caroline Kennedy spoke in 2013 at the hundredth birthday of the terminal, she joked as an aside that Mayor Bloomberg was probably relieved her mother wasn't around to challenge any of his controversial policies. The mayor and the room laughed good-naturedly, but immediately all who had known Jackie realized how much her spirit needs to be carried on.

An Alliance of Art and Politics

JACKIE AND THE JFK PRESIDENTIAL
LIBRARY AND MUSEUM

Declan Kiely is the Robert H. Taylor Curator of
Manuscripts and head of the Department of Literary and
Historical Manuscripts at the Morgan Library & Museum.

*A*FTER JOHN F. Kennedy's assassination, Jackie devoted
herself assiduously to protecting and promoting her husband's legacy. The most symbolic and eloquent expression of
her dedication and acute focus is the John F. Kennedy Presidential Library and Museum.

Competition for this prestigious but challenging project
was intense. But, as Arthur Herzog observed in the *New York
Times*, when the name of the architect was announced "there
was a long pause and people asked who and why." Jackie had
been instrumental in the selection of I. M. Pei, who was chosen

over the likes of Mies van der Rohe; John Carl Warnecke (designer of the Kennedy memorial at Arlington); Gordon Bunshaft of Skidmore, Owings & Merrill; Paul Rudolph; Louis Kahn; and Philip Johnson.

Responding to the raised eyebrows Pei's selection occasioned, Jackie remarked, "I suppose the choice was a little unorthodox. After all, some of the others were much better known. All those we considered are fine architects. But Pei! He loves things to be beautiful. People say, why didn't you find someone more established? We felt that Pei's best work, as John Kennedy's was in 1960, is yet to come."

In assessing the work of the architects under consideration, Jackie worked closely with her sister-in-law Jean Kennedy Smith and William Walton, the chairman of the federal Fine Arts Commission and a personal friend of the Kennedy family. They visited several cities to scrutinize the work of each architect and also interviewed them in their offices, asking the simple question, "What kind of library would you build?" As Walton recalled, "[The architects] laid bare their careers, their ideas, their hopes. It wasn't easy." Before making a final decision, Jackie conferred with Robert F. Kennedy, Edward Kennedy, Arthur Schlesinger Jr., Averell Harriman, and Supreme Court Justice Arthur Goldberg. "We were all nervous about saying who our personal choices were," said Jackie, "and delighted when it turned out that we had all come to the same conclusion."

Pei's own inclination, which clearly matched Jackie's vision, was "that it should be thought-provoking rather than awe-inspiring" but said all parties agreed, "it should be something that people will use—a living memorial."

It would take another fifteen years from the appointment of I. M. Pei in 1964, to the completion of the library at Columbia Point in the fall of 1979. Jackie's confidence in Pei's vision, and her support, were unshakeable. At the beginning of the project, in 1965, Jackie told the *New York Times*, "The one thing I am sure of is that Pei's work is growing. The library will grow too. At worst, we'll have a building the country can be proud of, though I have every hope it won't be just good, but great."

Without Jackie's unwavering focus the library may never have been completed. She spearheaded the fund raising—the total cost of $20.8 million was raised from public gifts and the Kennedy family—and worked indefatigably as the building project weathered planning controversies, site switching, and successive reprogramming.

The presidential library and museum was dedicated on October 20, 1979. As Ada Louise Huxtable wrote in her *New York Times* review, "the design by I. M. Pei and Partners is very good indeed—architecturally, symbolically and in the use of the arts of display." Huxtable concluded that the library represented "a giant step forward for this peculiarly American alliance of art and politics."

The Hemingway Collection

That alliance is epitomized by the presence of the Ernest Hemingway Collection, for within "this austere architectural drama" is the "exquisite, special room" that I. M. Pei promised Jackie he would create for that magnificent literary collection.

The president was a great admirer of "Papa" Hemingway's work and cited the novelist in the first sentence of *Profiles in Courage*: "This is a book about the most admirable of human virtues—courage. 'Grace under pressure,' Ernest Hemingway defined it."

When Hemingway shot himself in the summer after the inauguration, President Kennedy released a statement that paid tribute to the Nobel laureate's achievements: "Few Americans have had a greater impact on the emotions and attitudes of the American people than Ernest Hemingway.... He almost single-handedly transformed the literature and the ways of thought of men and women in every country in the world."

At the time of Hemingway's death a substantial portion of his personal and literary estate remained at Finca Vigía, his home in Cuba, where he wrote *The Old Man and the Sea* (1951). President Kennedy arranged an exception to the travel ban at the time for American citizens that allowed Mary Hemingway, Ernest's fourth wife and widow, to go to Cuba in order to reclaim some portable family property, including most of Hemingway's literary papers. The Cuban government had expropriated Finca Vigía and all of its remaining contents. Nevertheless, Mary met with Fidel Castro and, with his personal approval, was able to transport several crates of Hemingway's papers aboard a shrimp boat from Havana to Tampa, Florida.

In 1964, William Walton, who was also a close friend of the Hemingways, was aware that Mary was considering an appropriate institutional repository for her husband's papers. He prompted Mary to contact Jackie. At the conclusion of their discussions, Mary offered the Hemingway papers—which included manuscripts, letters, scrapbooks, notebooks, paintings, photographs, and memorabilia—to the John F. Kennedy Presidential Library and Museum.

Mary Hemingway had said that she wished to give the collection "to some place where [Hemingway] would be to himself and have a little personal distinction." It is also likely that Mary and Jackie, both tragically widowed, shared a deep, personal commitment to consolidating and memorializing their husbands' legacies.

In 1972, Mary, along with Hemingway's sons Jack, Patrick, and Gregory, formally donated the collection. As Jackie had predicted seven years earlier, the JFK Library did grow, and her focus on the acquisition of the Hemingway Collection makes it unique among presidential libraries. In announcing the gift of the Hemingway Collection, Jackie explained that the addition would "help to fulfill our hope that the Library will become a center for the study of American civilization, in all its aspects, in these years."

"Jackie chose [organizations] that were important to her and she stuck to them. If you spread yourself too thin, you can't do it all—she understood that. I think she'd say pick two or three things you're passionate about, that have real meaning to you, and work on those."

—BLAINE TRUMP

WHAT JACKIE TAUGHT US ABOUT
The Quest for Knowledge

CURIOSITY ABOUT A LARGER WORLD

"Learning is not attained by chance. It must be sought for with ardor and attended to with diligence."
—FIRST LADY ABIGAIL ADAMS, 1797–1801

JACKIE'S LIFELONG LOVE of learning prepared her for her greatest successes and was the springboard from which her confidence and direction emerged. An inquisitive little girl, she liked to learn about everything. In the summer, she would spend many sunny days with her sweet-natured Grandmother Bouvier in her highly manicured gardens at their East Hampton estate about two hours from New York City. It was in those glorious gardens, which won many horticultural prizes during the 1930s and 1940s, that Jackie eagerly learned the name of each flower and plant and how it grew. To her credit, she embraced all sources of knowledge throughout her life, including a formal education at first-rate schools, devotion to books, extensive travel, and an ongoing curiosity about the world at large.

Young children, particularly those growing up in dysfunctional households as Jackie and her younger sister Lee did, can be greatly influenced by grandparents who frequently have more time for them. As the marriage of Jackie's mother and father was growing more acrimonious, it was only natural for Jackie to look to her Bouvier grandparents, in particular, for stability and encouragement. The fact that the spacious Bouvier summer home was named Lasata, an Indian word for "place of peace," made it all the more fitting for Jackie to spend time there.

Jackie and Grampy Jack

Jackie's grandfather, John Vernou Bouvier Jr. ("Grampy Jack"), a distinguished New York lawyer and a graduate of Columbia Law School, was a passionate proponent of poetry and transmitted his enthusiasm to Jackie, his favorite grandchild. He would often compose a poem for one of his ten grandchildren and read it aloud to them after their Sunday lunch together. In turn, the grandchildren were routinely rewarded when they wrote an original poem for him. According to Jackie's sister, Lee, "He really adored her and I think felt that she had enormous potential in the field that he cared about, which was literary. They had quite a correspondence together, and many flowery letters were exchanged. I don't know if he got her interested in poetry, but she started to love poetry at an exceptionally early age and she gave him great pleasure. It was mutual, and it was very nice to watch them together. I think that if it hadn't been for this exceptional bond she had with my Grandfather Bouvier and my father that she never would have gained the particular strength and independence and individuality she had. Because we didn't have a very normal family . . ."

Grampy Jack shared his passion not only for poetry with his grandchildren, but also for plays and all forms of distinguished writing. Jackie's cousin, John H. Davis, recalled how his grandfather "in those pre-television days . . . would read aloud to us from Macauley and Shakespeare in his book-lined study and encourage us to read only the greatest works of literature."

Education of a First Lady

Unfortunately, his handsome son, Jackie's beloved father, John Vernou Bouvier III, known as Black Jack, had inherited little of his father's intellectual prowess. Indulged by his mother, Black Jack's interests were anything but literary and ranged from strong drink to women to gambling. He was even expelled from Phillips Exeter, his prep school, for placing bets. Intellectual and cultural pursuits bored him, and his academic record at Yale was not particularly stellar. However, he adored his two daughters and recognized Jackie's special gifts, encouraging her every step of the way.

Jackie's mother, Janet Lee Bouvier, was extremely intelligent and attended all the right WASP schools—Miss Spence's in New York City, one year at Sweet Briar College in Virginia, and another at Barnard College in New York—but never received a college degree. Most probably she was more focused on finding a socially acceptable husband than on pursuing academia. Cognizant of the value of education, she was diligent in monitoring her two daughters' schoolwork and always encouraged their artistic traits, including sketching. She also insisted that they memorize a poem for each holiday.

Janet's parents, James and Margaret Lee, who were estranged during Jackie's childhood, apparently didn't take much interest in Jackie's education. However, the impetus of Grampy Jack's love of literature, her father's unabashed praise, and her mother's diligent supervision, combined with Jackie's natural intelligence, appeared to be more than enough to launch her scholastically.

Jackie's formal quest for knowledge began at the age of five, when she learned how to read—a full year before she started school. She had an excellent memory, and reading came easier to her than to most children. The books she chose were not the usual children's classics such as *Honey Bunch* and the *Bobbsey Twins*. Instead, she read about her heroes—Robin Hood and the poet Lord Byron. She even tackled such adult works as Chekhov and G. B. Shaw, recalled her mother.

When Jackie was six, Janet found her reading a book of short stories by Chekhov, with complicated plots and long Russian names. "Did you understand all the words?" asked her mother. "Yes," she said, "except—what's a midwife?" Janet persisted. "Didn't you mind all those long names?" "No, why should I mind?"

Art history tomes were especially important to her and increased the lifelong joy she derived from drawing and painting. The noted historian Arthur M. Schlesinger Jr., added, "To her appreciation of the arts Jacqueline Kennedy added a passionate sense of history. She liked to know how things began and how they evolved, and her glamorous modernity was based on intense curiosity about the past." Her grandfather, John Vernou Bouvier Jr., was primarily responsible for Jackie's early interest in history, particularly that of France. He enthralled her with fanciful stories about the history of the Bouviers, describing their ancestors as titled aristocrats and members of the French parliament. Although years later Jackie would learn that much of this wasn't accurate, her grandfather's vivid descriptions inspired within Jackie a lifelong love of history and an appreciation of the lessons it taught.

The extensive knowledge of art and history that she

acquired over the years helped her to contribute substantially during her restoration of the White House with complete historical accuracy. Many years later, this knowledge also benefited New York City, as it was Jackie's influence that helped save several landmarks such as Grand Central Terminal and the Community House of St. Bartholomew's Episcopal Church.

In 1935, Jackie enrolled in the Chapin School, an exclusive school for young girls attended by more than three hundred daughters of well-to-do families. Founded in 1901 by Maria Bowen Chapin, part of the institution's philosophy is that each young woman should "shoulder her responsibility to make the world a better place"—advice that young Jackie embraced throughout her life. At Chapin, Jackie began the habit of reading virtually every book she could lay her hands on. Aside from the pleasure this gave her, reading also allowed her to escape from the pain of her parents' rapidly disintegrating marriage.

Along with being considered the brightest student at the Chapin School, Jackie was also seen as a mischievous child. Her mother's opinion was that Jackie was more intellectually advanced than her chronological age. "Her problem at Chapin was sheer boredom. Jackie would finish her classroom lessons before any of the other children and, lacking things to do, make a nuisance of herself. She could be audacious and demanding, even show-offy—a handful for those in charge of her," her mother proffered. For her entire life, Jackie would be restless if she didn't have something interesting to put her mind to.

It reached the point where Janet heard that Jackie was being sent regularly to the office of the headmistress, Miss Stringfellow. She confronted Jackie and asked her what happened in Miss Stringfellow's office. Jackie told her mother that ". . . Miss Stringfellow says a lot of things—but I don't listen."

Eventually the savvy headmistress, who was anxious to harness her prized student's intellectual capabilities, got Jackie to listen by tapping into her love for horses. Miss Stringfellow told Jackie that she was very much like a beautiful thoroughbred, strong and fast but not properly trained to race, whose talent would be useless as a racehorse.

"You can run fast. You have staying power. You're well built, and you have brains. But if you're not properly broken and trained, you'll be good for nothing." Understanding the merits of the metaphor, Jackie responded positively and ceased her rebellious behavior. Jackie would later say that Miss Stringfellow was "the first, great moral influence" in her life.

At one point, Miss Stringfellow told Janet, "I mightn't have kept Jacqueline—except that she has the most inquiring mind we've had in thirty-five years."

Jackie's after-school hours were filled with ballet and ballroom dancing lessons as well as riding instruction. Her mother carefully watched to see that her daughters' manners were up to par and instituted other lessons at the dining table as well. Janet, interested in improving Jackie and Lee's knowledge of French, insisted that they speak it at dinner. If they wanted the salt, they had to give their mother the French equivalent of the word before she would pass it. She even devised a game to perfect their fluency. Each child would be given ten matches, and whoever spoke an English word would have to forfeit a match. The child with the most matches at the end of the meal won.

In 1943, at age fifteen, Jackie wanted to put some distance between herself and her mother and decided to go to boarding school at Miss Porter's in Farmington, Connecticut, one of New England's most beautiful towns. Perhaps she needed space from her strong-willed mother, who constantly reminded her to hide her intelligence, as some men found it threatening. After all, why would parents tell a young girl it's important to study hard if it's going to work against her? Jackie didn't accept Janet's counsel for very long, and in a few short years she would find no reason to hide her love of learning.

Founded in 1843, Miss Porter's hadn't changed much when Jackie attended. A hundred years later it was still run as a "finishing school," as young women traditionally finished their education there, hardly ever going on to college. It still catered mostly to wealthy families who wanted their daughters to benefit from an environment that graduated young women who were both well educated and polished. The school emphasized good manners and the fact that it was still polite to curtsey at the appropriate time. To that end, rules and regulations were rather strict: no smoking, no drinking, no card playing, and limited visits by boys. In their spare time, students were not even allowed to read whatever they wanted—popular romantic novels were explicitly forbidden.

Farmington instructed its young ladies on the importance of "guts and gumption" and stressed that when a crisis came, you faced it head-on and handled it yourself without asking for the assistance of others. That same message was passed on to Nancy Tuckerman, Jackie's best friend from Chapin, who also had transferred to Farmington where they eventually shared a room. Tuckerman remembered that, unlike her schoolmates who tended to socialize in the evening after study hall, "Jackie seldom joined in, happily staying in her room, reading, writing poetry, or drawing. Popular among her classmates, by nature she was a loner." Farmington's headmaster, Ward Johnson, referred to Jackie as "this extraordinary girl" in reference to her high marks and unusual appreciation of art and history. Lily Pulitzer, a former classmate and now a fashion designer, said that Jackie seemed highly intelligent and that she "never saw her without a stack of books in hand, even when she wasn't studying. I had the distinct impression that in those days she preferred books to boys." Jackie, far more mature than most of the young men who asked her out and schooled by Black Jack to be wary of the wayward ways of men, deliberately put her social life on the back burner in favor of school work, poetry, art, riding, and other sports.

At Farmington, students were allowed to keep their own horses, and many did. Jackie, very much wanting to bring her mare, Danseuse, asked her mother if this would be possible. As the horse's upkeep would cost approximately $25 a month, Janet was reluctant to agree to what she considered an extravagance. Jackie wrote her grandfather a letter to see if he would pay for Danseuse's boarding. Unable to resist her charming plea, he granted her request, which was no doubt helped by the fact that she cleverly enclosed the latest poem she had written and asked for his critique, demonstrating that education could have many rewards.

Following her Grandfather Bouvier's lead, Jackie was also a straight-A student in school. While at Farmington, she joined the drama and riding clubs as well as contributed poems and cartoons for the school newspaper. In June 1947, at age eighteen, Jackie graduated from Miss Porter's near the top of her class, winning the Maria McKinney Memorial Award for Excellence in Literature, one of her favorite subjects along with art history.

"She was intellectually ahead of herself," recalls Noreen Drexel, whose cabana in Newport adjoined the Auchincloss's. "She wrote stories for children and read them to the children in the neighborhood. You had the sense that she could have been an excellent teacher or perhaps an important author."

Jackie, unlike her mother, felt that a college education was important and applied to Vassar, where she was immediately accepted. Founded in 1861 and considered a pioneer for women's education, Vassar is a highly selective, residential, liberal arts college. Now coeducational after opening its doors to men in 1969, it was an "all-girls" college when Jackie entered as a freshman in 1947.

It's easy to construe that Jackie, an independent thinker who liked to find her own answers, may have selected the college because Vassar women were recognized as a "breed apart" for their independence of thought and their inclination to "go to the source in search of answers." It must have inspired Jackie, given her lifelong interest in art, that part of the college's credo was that art should stand "boldly forth as an educational force." So strongly did the college believe in that thought that Vassar was the first college in the country to include an art museum among its facilities.

An excellent student who routinely made the Dean's List, Jackie was also awarded As for her ability in some of the courses acknowledged to be extremely difficult—the history of religion and a class in Shakespeare. So taken was she with the poetic words of *Antony and Cleopatra* that she memorized and recited large portions of the play. Those evenings when Grampy Jack read Shakespeare aloud to his grandchildren obviously had made an impression on her.

Throughout her life, Jackie believed in the power of words, so much so that she wrote, "Once you can express yourself, you can tell the world what you want from it. . . . All the changes in the world, for good or evil, were first brought about by words."

A Year Abroad

Jackie, like many other college students, wanted to go abroad for her junior year, but Vassar didn't offer a foreign-study program. She discovered on a bulletin board posting that Smith College offered a study program at the Sorbonne in Paris, and she received permission from the dean at Vassar to apply based on her high grades. After passing a French exam and writing an essay, Jackie was accepted by Smith.

Founded in 1253 for theology students without money, the Sorbonne stresses that its "international reputation has always placed it among Europe's most important universities." The fact that the school specialized in teaching French history and French literature to foreign students must have been especially appealing to Jackie. Along with its world-famous professors, she certainly must have been surprised by the fact that the university also has the dubious distinction of having sided with England in condemning Joan of Arc many centuries earlier.

The school offered housing for American students at Reid Hall, but Jackie chose to live with a local French family instead in order to immerse herself in French life. Far away from home and the very comfortable Auchincloss lifestyle, she entered a much different world. It was only four years after the city had been liberated from the Nazi occupation, and although there was a spirit of exuberance and rebirth among the citizens, there were numerous hardships as well. Everyday conveniences were scarce, with hot water and heating fuel in short supply. Meals consisted of simple soups and stews, and Jackie was allowed only one cold-water bath a week at the home of the aristocratic, but poor, family where she boarded.

In the fall of 1949, she began her courses at the university in French history and art history, both taught in French. She also took a course in photography, which undoubtedly came in handy several years later in her job as the Inquiring Photographer at the *Washington Times-Herald.* "I'm also a photographer and used a Leica [camera] at the Sorbonne," she told her prospective employer in 1952. In addition to her studies at the Sorbonne, she also added courses in diplomatic history at the École de Science Politique and art instruction at the École de Louvre.

Jackie found plenty of adventure in Paris, the city she would love for the rest of her life. Largely because of her French roots, however far removed, Jackie was truly at home in the city and immersed herself in its social, cultural, and intellectual life. She dated young, attractive Frenchmen and attended numerous society balls and parties with them as well as frequenting cafés and clubs. As improving her knowledge of the arts was important, she also visited museums and often went to the ballet, opera, and theater. On weekends and holidays, she explored different parts of the continent. Despite immersing herself so deeply in Parisian life, Jackie never allowed herself to be distracted from her studies.

It was in Paris that Jackie came of age intellectually and finally put aside her mother's admonition that men preferred beauty, not brains. "I learned not to be ashamed of a real hunger for knowledge, something I had always tried to hide," Jackie said about her year abroad. At the end of her scholastic year, her concentration paid off, and the Sorbonne awarded her a certificate of high achievement. "I never worked harder in my life," she later recalled.

Fluency with Foreign Languages

Upon returning to America, Jackie decided not to go back to Vassar, instead transferring to George Washington University. She graduated in 1951 with a bachelor's degree in French literature and a strong minor in art. Her year in France perfected her ability to speak French, adding to her fluency in Spanish and Italian. Her Vassar roommate, Edna Harrison, studied Spanish with her and recalled that Jackie excelled in it. ". . . She whizzed through the class, she got all A's and she was just trying to coach me through it."

Years later, Jackie's facility with foreign languages became a formidable weapon for the wife of a politician, personally charming world leaders and ethnic constituencies and especially voters for whom English was a second language. During her husband's senate campaign in 1958, Jackie appeared before nearly eight hundred people at the Michelangelo School in Boston's North End and spoke in perfect Italian on his behalf. When Jackie reached the podium, most of those present didn't know who she was, especially the Italians and the elderly, according to William De Marco, a longtime district leader for the Democratic Party, who was also present.

"But when she opened her mouth and introduced herself in Italian, fluent Italian may I say, as the wife of Senator Kennedy, all pandemonium broke loose. All the people went over and started to kiss her, and the old women spoke to her as if she was a native of the North End and I think her talk is actually what cemented the relationship between Senator Kennedy and the Italian-Americans of the district."

Jack and Jackie also appeared together at the Queen of the Rice Festival in Lafayette, Louisiana, in October 1959. Jackie addressed the crowd of 100,000 people, mostly French-speaking Cajuns, in her soft voice. "Bonjour, mes amis." The applause and screaming were deafening, according to campaign worker Edmund Reggie.

Reggie said that Jackie told the crowd in French that "she was very happy to be here in south Louisiana because her father had told her when she was a child that Louisiana was a little corner carved out of France . . . and she had a great love for France and since she herself was half [French] . . . that she was happy to see for herself that what her father said was true, that this was the beautiful part of France."

According to *Palm Beach Post* reporter Marilyn Murray Willison, Jackie's fluency with foreign languages made her a role model and an inspiration for a whole generation of baby boomers in the 1960s, especially if they were female and Catholic. "I went to a Catholic girls' high school in a small California town. There were photos of President and Mrs. Kennedy in every classroom. The nuns made no secret of the fact that they admired the Kennedys and felt that Jackie was the ultimate role model for teenage girls. Our little school offered Spanish, French and Latin and our teachers told us that learning languages would have lasting benefits just as it had for the polished, polyglot First Lady, whose language skills had helped her husband win the Presidential election. We were encouraged to continually use our brain and constantly strive for improvement."

A Sponge for Knowledge

Jackie remained a voracious reader throughout her life. As her friend Jayne Wrightsman remembers, "She finished as many as eight to ten books a week, on subjects of architecture, history and biography." Author Truman Capote, remarking on Jackie's reading habits, said, "She reads as much as anybody I know—a book a day isn't unusual for her."

Beyond pleasure and personal enrichment, the knowledge books provided her enabled Jackie to succeed in the major endeavors she undertook. She was so devoted to reading, and particularly the classics Grampy Jack had shared with her many years earlier, that she once said, "Read for escape, read for adventure, read for romance, but read the great writers. You will find to your delight that they are easier and more joy to read than the second-rate ones. They touch your imagination and your deepest yearnings, and when your imagination is stirred it can lead you down paths you never dreamed you would travel."

Jackie was a sponge for knowledge, and no matter the source, she never passed up an opportunity to learn a new skill or technique that interested her. She demonstrated this in a charming letter she sent in May 1963 to a society painter and craftsman who had painted some of the walls at "Wexford," her "beloved little house" that she and Jack were building in the Virginia countryside. ". . . It's a joy to see you work and to learn from you," she wrote. "You have been more than kind to me— and all your men so nice (one of them taught me how to marbleize with a cloth)—but needless to say, I don't think I will ever give you any competition!"

Travel particularly enriched Jackie's life. As a teenager, she had spent time in Europe visiting the great cities. France and all its historic glory, and especially Paris, with its magnificent churches, monuments, and buildings, deeply influenced her.

So completely captivated by Europe was she that she told friends, "I want to come back and soak it all up."

In November 2002, some fifty years after Jackie lived in Paris as a student at the Sorbonne, her daughter, Caroline, traveled there for the opening of the exhibit "Jacqueline Kennedy: The White House Years." Caroline commented, "Paris was the city that my mother loved and that inspired her throughout her life. Her passion for history guided and informed her work in the White House. It was a passion that came alive during the year she lived and studied in Paris."

As First Lady, Jackie circled the globe, visiting numerous countries—Canada, France, Austria, Venezuela, India, and Pakistan, among others. Because she was basically a scholar at heart, she carefully researched the history of each country and completely immersed herself in its culture before traveling there. This not only broadened her awareness, it made a lasting impression on some of the world's greatest leaders, including France's President de Gaulle and India's Prime Minister Nehru.

Thirst for Learning

Although Jackie frequently asserted that she had little interest in politics, she wanted to better understand her husband's world of politics and foreign relations. In 1954, she decided to take some courses in U.S. history and the development of civilization at Georgetown University. According to Harold Stephens, a journalist and author who attended classes with Jackie, it turned out to be a provocative decision, as special arrangements had to made for her to attend. According to Stephens, Father Frank Fadner, the Dean of the Foreign Service School at Georgetown, told the class that "this is not school policy but an exception, but we have a woman, the wife of a newly elected senator, who will be attending some of our classes." Stephens remembers that Georgetown was then "a snobbish school—no women, blacks or confessed Democrats, strong on fraternities, and little to do with sports. The announcement that a woman was coming to class wasn't well received."

Jackie was twenty-three at the time, and Stephens only a little older. "We were both outcasts at Georgetown, particularly in the Foreign Service School. She, because she was a female, and I because I was a high school dropout and former U.S. Marine who had somehow managed to get a political appointment from Ambassador Jefferson Caffery to attend the university. I was in my third year at Georgetown when Jackie Kennedy came into my history class. She was assigned the seat to my right. It seems odd but she appeared ordinary. Her skirt was below her knees and she wore a sweater and low-heeled shoes and socks. In fact, no one among the student body seemed to notice her. Maybe she was trying to blend in." Although Jackie was an excellent student, Stephens recalls, "She seemed more interested in talking about art than political theory."

Once, during a long break between classes, Jackie invited him to walk with her to a favorite shop on M Street where prints sold for just two dollars. "She knew exactly where to look," says Stephens. "I truly believe this was the true Jackie, the Bohemian."

While Jackie may have preferred art to political affairs, her belief in the value of knowledge and her desire to become an asset to her husband inspired her to learn all she could about his world.

Astronaut John Glenn observed Jackie's intellectual breadth up close as First Lady. "Whenever there was a discussion going on about the Far East or Mideast or Russia, or any world affairs, she was very well informed and could hold her own in any conversation. She never made any public knowledge of this and it wasn't the way most people viewed her. Behind the scenes, once you got beyond this veneer that she had been pigeonholed in, you realized this."

Although she was in her late thirties when she married Aristotle Onassis in 1968 and moved to Greece, her thirst for learning was as great as always. She completely engrossed herself in Greek culture, learning the language; studying the history, literature, and art of Greece; and even mastering the native syrtaki dance. Robert Pounder, a professor of classics at Vassar, whom she met at a party some twenty years later, was amazed at how much Jackie knew about contemporary and ancient Greece as well as Greek archaeology. "We discussed the excavations at Samothrace. She had all the landscape and excavations in her memory."

Unlike Jackie, Aristotle Onassis didn't particularly relish the idea of spending an evening curled up with a good book. Indeed, he complained that "All Jackie does is read." Onassis's comment was not only accurate but eerily prescient. Shortly after his death, Jackie's love of literature led her to accept a job in publishing. It must have given Jackie great satisfaction to get paid for something that for years had been her most pleasurable pastime.

Her work as an editor was extremely rewarding for Jackie and, in many ways, a fitting culmination of all that had interested her throughout her life. Not only did she have the opportunity to be surrounded by others who cherished the written word and to be an integral part of the creative process, but it was also a chance for her to continue learning through exposure to new ideas and the people and places that fascinated her. At the same time, the breadth of her richly diverse knowledge, acquired throughout a lifetime of exploration, was an extremely valuable quality for an editor to have. "What I like about being an editor," she once said, "is that it expands your knowledge and heightens your discrimination. Each book takes you down another path . . ."

Betty Prashker, the editorial director at Doubleday to whom Jackie reported, found her to be very intelligent and shrewd. "She understood what people would want to read about and, most importantly, she had access to the world. Anyone was just one phone call away. This was a formidable asset for an editor and she made the most of it."

Prashker also remembers the practical side of Jackie's thinking. "Although she had tremendous persistence, she knew when to let go. If something wasn't going to work, she dropped it. In the midst of all this, she had a great sense of humor and always saw the irony of a situation."

There were people who had known Jackie previously who discovered a new side to her when she became an editor. "I knew Jackie for many years," said Marc Riboud, a photographer whose book, *Capital of Heaven*, was edited by Jackie. "But it was only when we worked together that I started really to know her. We were now accomplices, with one goal: the success of a book. Then, beyond the surface brilliance, I discovered an intense seriousness and an astonishing strength of will. With intelligence and passion, she demanded the highest quality."

Joannie Danielides, a New York communications expert and then a graduate student in art history working part-time at the Metropolitan Museum of Art, remembers the day Jackie visited the museum's Costume Institute in 1976 regarding a book she was editing. "I was a kid in my twenties and Mrs. Onassis wanted to meet with my boss who headed up the slide library. Jackie was editing a book called *In the Russian Style* and needed to review some of our slides for possible inclusion in the manuscript. My strongest memory of her was her confidence in asking lots of questions in order to understand all the details. She taught me you can't be an expert in everything; however you can always empower yourself by not being afraid to ask questions."

That Jackie would choose to return to work is a tribute to her recognition that she needed to be intellectually challenged in order to feel whole and complete. It's all the more amazing after her spectacular reign as First Lady and later as the wife of a megabillionaire that she would choose to take a job at a lower rung in the publishing industry.

As feminist writer Gloria Steinem noted, "Given the real options of using Kennedy power or of living an Onassis-style life, how many of us would have the strength to return to our own careers—to choose personal work over derived influence? In the long run, her definition of work may be more helpful to women than the conventional kind of power she has declined."

Stephen Rubin, president and publisher of Doubleday, said, "[F]ew people understood how committed and talented she was at the work she chose to do. . . . Many were surprised to hear that she actually came to the office, attended meetings and worked hard. . . . Making money wasn't what fueled her passion; publishing good, interesting books motivated her. And such was her uncanny instinct that many of her projects became truly popular while also retaining the formidable quality for which she was famed."

This passion for learning stayed with Jackie all her life, through her marriage to John Kennedy and as the First Lady of the land, as widow and mother, later as the wife of Aristotle Onassis, and finally as an unmarried, independent working woman. The fact that Jackie would spend the last years of her life with Maurice Tempelsman, a man who valued learning and literature as much as she did, was a fitting ending to the life of a woman whose intellectual curiosity rivaled that of the world's fascination with her.

What Jackie Taught Us

With her passionate, lifelong love of learning, Jackie taught us that knowledge can be a source of power and a tool of discovery, as well as an oasis of pleasure and comfort. As a child, she turned to books as a safe haven from family turmoil. Throughout her life, reading provided a wondrous playground for exploration and enjoyment as well as a welcome refuge from a life that too often was fraught with disappointment and pain.

Jackie's insatiable hunger for knowledge was constant and never fully satisfied. She was as eager to learn everything she could about her favorite pastimes as she was to understand those things that were completely new to her. It was Jackie's knowledge of history and the arts, for example, that formed the foundation for one of her greatest triumphs as First Lady: the restoration of the White House.

When Jackie lacked knowledge on a given subject, she was not satisfied until she had acquired it. As the young bride of John Fitzgerald Kennedy, a rising U.S. senator, Jackie went so far as to return to college to take courses in foreign service and international relations because she wanted a better understanding of her husband's world. And later, as a devoted and loving mother, she studied the techniques and advice of noted child-rearing experts, especially Dr. Benjamin Spock. As First Lady, she made it a point to learn as much as she could about a country's history and culture before she visited it. While many foreign dignitaries were dazzled by Jackie's style and charm, it was her mastery of foreign languages and a deep knowledge of world history that truly won both their hearts and their respect.

When Jack Kennedy, whose appreciation of beautiful women was well known, first met Jackie, he was immediately drawn to her as much for her love of books, her thirst for knowledge, and her desire to learn as he was attracted by her unique beauty. Her enthusiasm for knowledge was infectious, and both her children gratefully credited her for inspiring their love of literature and learning.

Our lives are filled with multiple opportunities and reasons to pursue knowledge. Our challenge is to look for it in the best possible places. With the advent of technological marvels that allow us to communicate rapidly, coupled with an array of entertainment and amusement choices at our fingertips, it's easy to become passive consumers of knowledge. In doing so, however, we risk the danger of simply filling ourselves with the thoughts, ideas, and even values of others. Jackie didn't allow this to happen, and we shouldn't, either. When we take personal responsibility for pursuing knowledge, we open our lives to boundless opportunities. By keeping our mental curiosity vibrant, we will continue to move forward.

Former First Lady Eleanor Roosevelt said it best when she wrote, "If you stop learning, you stop living in any vital and meaningful sense!"

A Passion for Words

Lynne Olson is the author of *Citizens of London*
and *Those Angry Days*.

WHEN JOHN AND Jacqueline Kennedy entered the White House in 1961, a whole new world opened up for me. Not yet in my teens, I knew I wanted to do something with my life, something more than getting married and having children, but I had no idea what that was. It wasn't until President Kennedy's now-famous challenge to Americans in his inaugural speech—"Ask not what your country can do for you, ask what you can do for your country"—that I began to see beyond my own limited horizons. Growing up in Colorado, I was a child of the West, but, inspired by the president's summons to public service, I vowed that one day I would live and work in Washington—and take part in the exciting world he was creating there.

Jacqueline Bouvier Kennedy inspired me, too. I was fascinated by her beauty, elegance, and glamour, as so many others were. Yet, in a curious way, even though we had seemingly nothing in common, she also reminded me of myself. Like me, she had been passionate about reading since early childhood, retreating into her room with a book whenever she could and escaping into another world. The power of words was extremely important to her, as it was to me; so was the joy of learning something new. All her life, she possessed an endlessly inquiring mind.

When I graduated from college, I did go to Washington, to work for a congressman whose idealism and devotion to public service reminded me of what had excited me so much about JFK. It wasn't long, however, before my curiosity about the larger world lured me into a journalism career, which included stints in San Francisco, New York, Moscow, and a return to Washington. A generation before, a young Jacqueline Bouvier, eager to establish her independence, had sought a journalism career of her own. In the early 1950s, however, it was extremely difficult for women to succeed in the male-dominated newspaper world, and Jacqueline had to settle for a job as Inquiring Photographer for the *Washington Times-Herald*. (With her spirit of adventure and love of travel, I've always thought she would have made a fabulous foreign correspondent.)

When I embarked on a second career as a writer of narrative nonfiction books, I felt I had developed yet another connection with her. While in our forties, we both had returned to our love for books and made it the centerpiece of our lives. In 1975, fueled by her intense intellectual curiosity and her determination to find fulfillment on her own terms, Jacqueline Kennedy became a book editor at Viking, moving later to Doubleday. It is not surprising that she turned out to be brilliant at her new vocation. For the rest of her life—some nineteen years—she shepherded dozens of books to publication with her customary skill, grace, and dedication. Her authors were devoted to her. I only wish I had been one of them.

A Real Hunger for Knowledge

Jennifer J. Raab is the president of Hunter College,
City University of New York.

THE IMAGES OF Jackie that endure—especially from that tragic day in Dallas—are so powerful in our collective memory that they tend to overshadow the real person and the extraordinary legacy she left our nation.

As a college student in her junior year studying abroad at the Sorbonne in Paris, Jackie saw firsthand the historical and beautiful monuments of Europe, particularly those in Paris. This left on her an indelible impression of how important historic preservation is to our cultural psyche. From restoring the elegance of the White House to helping preserve America's cultural heritage—especially the rescue of Grand Central in New York and Lafayette Square in Washington—to her continuing support for the arts, she enriched the lives of her fellow citizens in countless ways.

It is telling that she grew up in an era when young women were still being told to limit their educations and submerge their intellects so as not to repel young men, which explains why the public Jackie often seemed so modest, even shy at times. It is equally telling that she chose to ignore that advice and pursue a lifetime of learning. From childhood, she was a voracious reader; she mastered French (among other languages); she was fascinated by history; she became a leading advocate for American culture.

Looking back years later at her junior year in France, she said it was there that "I learned not to be ashamed of a real hunger for knowledge, something I had always tried to hide." That hunger continued until the end and was underscored by her son John Jr.'s statement announcing her death. "My mother died," he said, "surrounded by her friends and her family and her books." The inclusion of books among the things she loved and wanted near her provides a deep insight into who she truly was and what makes her so uniquely important.

It is an importance that has touched my life in many ways. As a young woman growing up when the place of women in American society was undergoing sweeping changes, I and others could look to her as a model of strength and independence—someone who proved it was possible to be famous, glamorous, and serious at the same time.

I shared along with my fellow New Yorkers the pleasure of knowing she was one of us, and we all applauded her leading role in the campaign to preserve the architectural treasure that is Grand Central. That battle had a direct impact on my life because it led to the U.S. Supreme Court's upholding the constitutionality of New York's Landmarks Preservation Commission, which years later I was appointed to lead. One of the projects we were proud to work on involved the restoration of Grand Central's magnificent interior.

Now as the president of the city's largest public college I appreciate more deeply than ever Jackie's hunger for learning. For everyone who is engaged in providing high-quality education at a price families can afford and for everyone who believes America's ability to compete in the global economy depends on a highly educated workforce, Jackie's lifelong love of learning—her quest for knowledge—is a continuing inspiration.

Jackie once reportedly said, "Maybe one day they will realize there is something underneath that pillbox hat." Indeed, we do, Jackie!

*"She was always reading! That's the image
I have when I think of her."*

—CAROLINE KENNEDY

What Jackie Taught Us About
Men and Marriage

"THAT CERTAIN SOMETHING"

"The first time you marry for love, the second for money, and the third for companionship."

—Attributed to Jacqueline Kennedy Onassis

W HAT WAS IT about Jacqueline Bouvier that enabled her to conquer two men considered by many to be among the world's most desirable? Extremely powerful, neither was hardly like the boy next door. Her first husband—tall, handsome, and rich—John Fitzgerald Kennedy, became the thirty-fifth president of the United States and swiftly made his mark on the entire world, particularly on women. Hollywood starlets, fresh-faced debutantes, and international beauties were at his beck and call. Her second, Aristotle Onassis, was charismatic, cunning, and also hugely fascinating to women. One of the world's wealthiest men, he offered an airline, an island in

Greece, and a 303-foot yacht as part of his marital dowry. Both men thought Jackie had "that certain something" that they couldn't do without—"beauty, charm, charisma, style, any or all of the above," as Igor Cassini, the society columnist, described her. But many other women also had these attributes. What gave Jackie her edge?

Lessons from Her Father's Knee

Part of Jackie's success with men can be traced to the lessons she learned from her handsome father, John (Jack) Vernou Bouvier III. Jack Bouvier was the parent whom Jackie resembled most in looks. He was a dashing figure—six feet tall and slim with a muscular body, complemented by sensual, full lips, piercing blue eyes, wide-set Bouvier style, and a thick head of dark hair he kept immaculately lacquered down. He was an elegant dresser and moved in such an easy way that he invariably drew attention to himself, as much for his looks as his posture. With a huge zest for life and love, Black Jack was a heartbreaker, and he knew it.

Although Jack Bouvier married his wife, Janet Lee, with all good intentions, he had no plans to change his womanizing ways. Irresistible to women, his relationships were typically one-night stands, and any woman to whom he was attracted had to have something special. Jackie absorbed his views on women and began to pattern herself accordingly.

An experienced ladies' man, Black Jack had a particular interest in women's fashions and would often take his daughters shopping at such chic New York clothing stores as Saks Fifth Avenue, Bonwit Teller, and Bergdorf Goodman. He stressed to Jackie and her younger sister, Lee, that regardless of the looks a woman was born with, it was the way she put herself together that was important. Even a plain woman, he told them, can look attractive if she dresses well.

Black Jack taught his daughters other valuable lessons that would serve them well in the years to come. Just as an actress learns how to make a proper entrance on stage, Jack schooled Jackie and Lee on the fine art of entering a room. To be noticed in a crowd, he advised, walk to the center of a room, put a dazzling smile on your face, and keep your chin up. Don't let your eyes dart around the room. Never act as if you're looking for someone; they should be looking for you. Be choosy about whom you speak to. Don't be overly friendly and appear too eager. That scares men off, he warned.

Black Jack personified charm with a capital C and passed this trait on to Jackie. The magnetic pull of Jackie's personality easily drew people to her. Most likely it was Black Jack who taught Jackie the "lighthouse look." According to one of her biographers, "When Jackie found a man she wanted, she became a lighthouse, charming everyone in sight." Gore Vidal, the author whose stepfather, like Jackie's, was Hugh D. Auchincloss Jr., remarked, "Jackie doesn't look around the room trying to see who else is there. She zeroes in on you with those wide-set eyes and listens to you with a shining, breathless intensity."

Her stockbroker father trained Jackie that the world revolved around money—that if you have something someone else wants, a price tag comes with it. Jack Kennedy soon learned that when he wanted Jackie to do something, he had to bargain for it. Pierre Salinger, the White House press secretary, once asked Jackie to meet with a delegation of Girl Scouts who were visiting the White House. She told him that it wasn't her problem, that it was Jack's. When Salinger brought this to President Kennedy's attention, Jack said, "Just give me a minute and I'll straighten this out." When he came back, he was smiling and said Jackie agreed to do it. Amazed, Salinger asked, "How did you do it?" Jack replied, "It cost me." Salinger questioned, "A new dress?" "No," Kennedy answered. "Worse than that, two symphonies."

Along with schooling her in the fine art of negotiating with men, Black Jack also passed on to Jackie the advantage of not appearing too easily available. When you receive an invitation, don't feel any pressure to accept, he would caution. Instead, say that you'll have to let them know. Then when you do show up, it will make a bigger impression. Black Jack often used this technique on his own family, telling his mother or father, as well as his brother or sisters, "We'll try," when they invited him to a family gathering. When he and his daughters finally showed up, everyone was so pleased to see that they could make it.

It was while she was in school at Miss Porter's that Jackie began practicing in earnest what Black Jack preached. Although extremely popular, she turned down most invitations from young men who asked her out. Jackie felt no hesitation in putting her schoolwork first and her social life last. Mature for her age, it's not too hard to imagine that she found these young men boring. Telling her classmates that she didn't intend to be a housewife, the furthest thing from Jackie's mind at the time was marriage, especially to a conventional man.

Jackie made her debut in the fall of 1947 and became more popular than ever, especially when Igor Cassini named her "Debutante of the Year" and said she reflected "everything the leading debutante should be." Cassini's nationally syndicated column, "Cholly Knickerbocker," was widely read, and Jackie's selection gave her instant celebrity status in the East Coast establishment. Privately Cassini admitted that he usually chose prettier and flashier girls, but "I felt something very special in her, an understated elegance. Although shy and extremely private, she stood out in a crowd." Jackie's legend began to build.

Jackie's father also taught her to be suspicious of men, not to assume that they were perfect gentlemen, and warned her not to give too much away, especially physically. As Jackie was born before the sexual revolution, in an era when a woman's virginity before marriage was supposedly mandatory, it was easy to follow her father's advice.

Her cousin, John H. Davis, remembers that Jackie "didn't play hard to get—she was impossible to get." He added that young men from Princeton, Harvard, and Yale would invariably ask him, "Hey, what's wrong with that Debutante-of-the-Year cousin of yours? She doesn't put out." Or "What's the story on your Queen Deb cousin? You can't get even halfway to first base with her." Davis credits Black Jack for Jackie's tantalizing effect on men. "Her father helped make her that way. He had written and admonished her many times not to forget that 'all men are rats' and that it was 'fatal' to make herself seem 'available' or 'easy.' 'Always keep them guessing,' he would tell her."

Jackie absorbed that advice, not only keeping the men in her life guessing but her adoring public as well. As First Lady she gave few interviews, keeping to that policy for the remainder of her life, even refusing to write her memoirs. "I want to live my life, not record it," she remarked. Her reticence to reveal her every thought or explain her every action is in refreshing contrast to current celebrity tell-alls that give us more information than we ever care to know. Jackie felt no compunction to explain herself, stating, "The river of sludge will go on and on. It isn't about the real me. I want to savor life, not write about it. I'd rather spend my time feeling the mist of the ocean up at Martha's Vineyard."

By his example, Black Jack showed Jackie that it was far wiser to be with people who enhanced your life rather than "bores" who added nothing to it. Once, when he was walking with his daughters in Central Park, he noticed an older woman who showed signs of wanting to chat approaching them. "Go tell her to jump in the lake," said Jack, who could not abide bores.

Heeding her father's advice, Jackie was extremely selective about whom she spent time with. As First Lady, she frequently avoided such ceremonial duties as meeting with congressional wives, mid-level diplomats, and even a delegation of foreign students, often recruiting Lady Bird Johnson to stand in for her. Instead, Jackie would mostly use the time to be with her family, or to sometimes attend a cultural event, or even go fox hunting.

Reserving Her Magic for Men

Black Jack loved both his daughters, but there was no doubt that Jackie was the apple of his eye. Spoiled by his mother, who treated him as if he could do no wrong, he thought his daughters were perfect, too. He left the disciplining of Jackie and Lee to his wife, Janet, who had rigid rules and strict standards of behavior. Given this treatment, Jackie probably viewed men as warm and loving while women, especially her mother, were critical and impossible to please.

It's not surprising that her cousin John H. Davis recalled that "among her Bouvier cousins, she preferred the males over the females." This preference for male companionship was to last throughout Jackie's life. Both men and women admired her, but she was far more comfortable with men. Recognizing that this was part of her makeup, Jackie didn't try to resist it. Unlike her mother, she studiously avoided ladies' luncheons, bridge games, and charity committees.

Jackie didn't have a close network of contemporary female friends, and as First Lady, she tended to form friendships with women who acted as mentors, teaching her about the nuances of fine French furniture or the intricate aspects of landscape planning. She reserved her special magic for the males in her life. In her later years, she appeared more relaxed in the company of women, but she continued to look to men to provide the support she craved.

"Jackie had always resisted cultivating friendships with other women," remarked Lem Billings, a close friend of Jack's since their prep school days at Choate. "She reflected an aura of fragility which seemed to attract men more than women, and which at the same time reduced every man she met to pure jelly."

Few Men Could Resist Her Charms

Jackie's vulnerability had far-reaching appeal, leaving few men immune to her charms, regardless of race, religion, or politics. Fortunately for Jackie, this extended to Andre Meyer, a legendary venture capitalist and senior partner of the powerful Wall Street firm Lazard Freres. Frequently called the "Picasso of Banking," Meyer was a trusted adviser of the Kennedys and counted powerful figures like President Lyndon B. Johnson, CBS television founder William Paley, and the publisher of the *Washington Post*, Katharine Graham, among his friends. After her husband died, Jackie became very concerned about money and turned to Meyer for counsel. The financier, captivated by Jackie's charm and vulnerability, was mesmerized by her and, according to Madeleine Malraux, wife of the French minister of culture and a close friend of the financier, "He must surely have been in love with her. He thought she was *extraordinary*." It must have appealed to Jackie that the man *Fortune* magazine called "the most important investment banker in the Western world" would take such an interest in her life, not only managing her investments, but advising her on real estate, her children's schools, and even her love life.

When she decided to marry Aristotle Onassis, Meyer was bitterly opposed. "He's not good enough for you, Jackie. If you marry Onassis, you will topple from your position at the pinnacle of society." Although he was hurt and angry that she did not listen to him, Jackie later made peace with Meyer and he remained devoted to her throughout his life. On his deathbed, his last words to his good friend, Gianni Agnelli, one of the world's most successful industrialists, were to take good care of Jackie—"Make sure Jackie's all right." The fact that these two titans of business would be discussing Jackie's welfare as one of them lay dying speaks volumes about her effect on men.

Even journalists who prided themselves on their objectivity and would bridle at the thought of ever being susceptible to outside influences could fall under Jackie's spell. Best-selling author Theodore H. White was one of them. Publicly admitting that his famous *Life* magazine essay, in which he portrayed the Kennedy administration as "the days of Camelot" was flawed, he implied he was trying to please Jackie.

White knew that Jackie's description of a heroic John Kennedy admiring the words of a Broadway show tune, "Don't let it be forgot, that once there was a spot, for one brief shining moment there was Camelot," was at best fanciful, and at worst fabricated. Giving Jackie the benefit of the doubt, he reasoned that she wasn't asking for that much after all she'd been through. At her urging, he included the Camelot reference and even allowed Jackie to view and edit the draft of his article before he submitted it to the magazine.

". . . there was something extremely compelling about her at that moment," recalled White. "She could have sold me anything from an Edsel to the Brooklyn Bridge."

Jackie enchanted men from all walks of life, including some she didn't intend to. Celebrity photographer Ron Galella was one of them. Bronx-born and fresh out of the Air Force, Galella, a pioneer of "paparazzi" photography, was eager to earn a living. His specialty was snapping photographs of celebrities in their most unguarded moments. Always ready with his camera, he never left home without three fully loaded Nikons. His aggressive techniques in pursuing his quarry led to much-publicized scuffles with such superstars as Frank Sinatra, Paul Newman, and Marlon Brando, who punched him in the jaw.

Completely transfixed by the former First Lady, Galella turned his full attention to Jackie and her children. He doggedly stalked her every step, leaping over hedges, sneaking up on her on the street, and even hiding behind a coat rack in a Chinese restaurant to catch her off-guard. He went so far as to date her maid and pry her for details about Jackie's schedule. To prevent Jackie from recognizing him, he used a variety of disguises including wigs and mustaches. He even put on a scuba diving suit and prowled the waters off the Greek island of Skorpios in order to catch her on film. Attempting to foil his efforts, Jackie tried her own tricks to throw Galella off. Knowing editors wouldn't pay him as much for a photo if it didn't show her eyes, she often wore her dark sunglasses on the street. Jackie also tried wearing black, which doesn't photograph well. Sometimes she put her hand in front of her face to deliberately lessen the value of a picture. Yet the more she tried to elude him, the more he fixated on her. According to *Artforum* magazine, "Galella wooingly stalked Jackie Kennedy Onassis for years. His gaze-lust for her was so intense that any Galella picture of a Kennedy is, by magic default, a portrait of Jackie."

Although photographing Jackie provided Galella with a steady income, he was admittedly somewhat in love with her. As a sign of his respect for her, he always wore a coat and tie when he wanted to photograph her. In describing one of his encounters with Jackie, he gushed, "I'll always remember wandering Central Park on fall afternoons and all of a sudden finding her like a diamond in the grass." Adding to this romanticized description, he went on to praise her, lavishly saying that she not only has "beauty, wealth and glamour [but] she is sensitive, poetic and independent. Millions of people never get enough of her." According to author Kitty Kelley, "All of Galella's 4,000 photographs of Jackie showed her looking exquisitely beautiful. Not one was unflattering. He never photographed her smoking or drinking, and always took his pictures in bright light to camouflage her grey teeth and soften the wrinkles around her eyes. Each picture showed an undisguised love of his subject."

Windblown Jackie, one of Galella's most famous photographs, shows Jackie striding purposefully down the street on a fall afternoon in New York. Gloriously glamorous even in casual dress, Jackie's long, trim legs were encased in perfectly cut tight, tie-dyed jeans topped with a fashionable close-fitted knitted sweater that showed off her slim midriff to perfection. Catching her off-guard, Galella's photo shows Jackie with her head slightly turned and her famously luxuriant hair blown across her face. She has a half, but expectant, smile on her face. Sensual and confident-looking, the photo shows Jackie at her most appealing self. Galella said, "Da Vinci had his Mona Lisa and I have my *Windblown Jackie.* The smile on the Mona Lisa is the beginning of a smile. Likewise my photo of Jackie shows her just as her smile starts. When the teeth are showing, the peak of the smile, and the moment is over." This startlingly beautiful photo of Jackie and thousands of others that Galella took are some of the most visible reminders of Jackie's enduring legacy.

According to fashion designer Tom Ford, "Ironically, the very photographs that Mrs. Onassis resisted were the ones that made her an icon. . . . It was the grainy black and white shots taken through a telephoto lens, the sequences of her playing with her children in Central Park, that turned the former Jacqueline Kennedy into the mysterious Jackie O."

Jackie's ability to persuade others—especially men—to see things her way eventually enabled her to prevail in the highly controversial court battle with Galella, who had violated a restraining order to stay at least twenty-five feet away from her and thirty feet from her children. Her legal team quickly discovered that Jackie would be a formidable witness in the courtroom.

"Most witnesses need training before they testify," said Charles Berry, a New York City lawyer who was then a young attorney working on the case, "but she had an innate sense of how to conduct herself in the courtroom and didn't need much coaching at all." She completely captivated Irving Ben Cooper, the oldest active judge on the federal bench who came very close to throwing Galella in jail for contempt. Berry added, "I was impressed by her intelligence and manner. She understood the power of speaking softly, which commands the listener's attention. The courtroom was riveted when she testified."

Ed Reilly, the lead attorney representing Jackie on the case, was devoted to her, Berry remembered, and utterly dedicated to the cause of protecting the privacy of the most famous woman in the world. She was grateful to Reilly not only for the success his team achieved in the proceeding (as a result of which Galella agreed never to photograph her again) but also for the arrangements he made to get her in and out of the courthouse without more pictures. While Galella's lawyer Marvin Mitchelson gave press conferences to disappointed reporters on the front steps of the courthouse, her nondescript station wagon slipped quietly into and out of a basement entrance usually reserved for judges and criminals, and she avoided another unwanted onslaught from the press.

Although defeated in court, Galella lost none of his adoration and respect for Jackie. Asked in a newspaper interview in 2002 who was his favorite subject to photograph, he replied, "Jackie was the most interesting because No. 1, she was mobile like a deer—always running and never stopping to pose. That made it a greater challenge. Jackie just kept on doing things, and I like people doing things and my pictures show that. She was my ideal subject. I think she loved it."

Jackie's appeal to men was decidedly bipartisan, and this was no more apparent than in her relationship with Henry Francis du Pont, a prominent Republican and founder of the Winterthur Museum in Delaware. Aside from being one of the country's wealthiest men, du Pont, at age 81, was acknowledged to be the world's number-one expert on American antiques. An extremely knowledgeable collector, he had turned his home in Delaware into a museum.

Determined that the restoration of the White House would be a success, Jackie made up her mind to recruit du Pont as chairman of the newly formed Fine Arts Committee. Du Pont, whose primary responsibility would be to direct the efforts of the group in locating suitable antiques as well as raise the necessary money to purchase them, readily agreed to chair the committee, obviously charmed by Jackie and swayed by her managerial skills.

Jackie managed to remain in du Pont's good graces over the coming months, even when she insisted on having her own way as to how the restoration proceeded. However, when du Pont noticed a still life hanging in one of the White House drawing rooms, he could not help but comment on what was to him an obvious mistake. Reminding Jackie and Susan Mary Alsop, another committee member, as to the proper placement of such paintings, he asked, "Ladies, surely you are aware that still lifes are only for dining rooms?" Without a hint of disagreement, Jackie replied in her trademark breathless voice, "Oh Mr. du Pont, it just shows how little we know. Goodness, we are lucky to have you to teach us what to do. The still life will come down immediately."

Satisfied that Jackie respected his scholarship, du Pont expected the painting to be removed, and it was—for a while. Unbeknownst to him, Jackie put the painting back in the same location shortly after he left. The next time du Pont was in the White House, he found himself in the same drawing room, again with Jackie and Susan Mary Alsop, and noticed that the painting was back in its original location. Du Pont, showing not the slightest hint of disapproval, looked up at the painting and said to Mrs. Alsop, "Jackie really does have a remarkably good eye. Everything looks splendid." Jackie had challenged the elder statesman of the antiques world and ended up with him complimenting her in the process. Extremely self-confident, she felt no necessity to engage a person she wanted something from in a meaningless confrontation.

Jackie's charms reached across oceans and even touched

Nikita Khrushchev, the premier of the Soviet Union and, at the time, America's most feared enemy. Short, fat, and balding with a steely glare, Khrushchev had a chilling effect on people, and most were careful not to incur his wrath, particularly because the Soviets had hinted at setting off a nuclear war that was capable of annihilating its enemies. When President Kennedy and Jackie traveled to Vienna, Austria, to meet with the Soviet leader, Kennedy was extremely apprehensive, having been warned that Khrushchev would try to prey on any perceived weakness and would jump at an opportunity to put him on the defensive. The diplomatic staffs from both the American and Soviet sides were understandably nervous about this historic meeting.

When a photographer suggested that Khrushchev shake Kennedy's hand, the feisty premier winked at Jackie and said through his interpreter, "I'd like to shake her hand first." Later that evening at the state dinner, guests observed Jackie, wide-eyed and smiling in her sequined shell-pink chiffon dress, leaning close to Khrushchev, deep in conversation. So taken was the Soviet leader with Jackie that the Associated Press described their encounter as "the tough and often belligerent Communist leader looked like a smitten schoolboy when the ice thaws along the Volga in springtime." Khrushchev, dazzled by Jackie's appearance, said that the dress she was wearing was "beautiful."

When he began to brag about the number of schoolteachers in the Ukraine, Jackie turned her lovely white shoulders toward him and interrupted his diatribe by saying, "Oh, Mr. Chairman, don't bore me with statistics!" Soviet aides, knowing of Khrushchev's terrible temper, jumped to their feet, thinking he would explode with anger. Instead, he paused and began laughing. With eight brief words, Jackie accomplished what few people in the world could have. She both deflated and at the same time charmed a man whose very name invoked terror.

Jackie had the ability to captivate complete strangers within a few minutes of meeting them. Luis Rey, a designer at McMillen Inc., one of the country's leading interior design firms, worked with Jackie on the rooms used for private functions at the John Fitzgerald Kennedy Library in Boston. Although he had never met her before, he said, "Within five minutes, I saw that she had the kind of magic that made you fall in love with her. I can't define exactly what it was, but she made me feel completely at ease, as though what I had to say was extremely important to her." He remembers that she was "a fantastic listener" and instantly grasped his design concepts.

Marry First for Love

Jackie's magnetic effect on men attracted a widely diverse group of suitors. Each fulfilled a particular need at a particular time in her life. An undocumented quote often attributed to Jackie Kennedy advises that, "The first time you marry for love, the second for money, and the third for companionship." Whether or not Jackie actually said this doesn't really matter, because it turned out that it was almost exactly what she did. Without question, Jack Kennedy, her first husband, was the love of her life, and when they married, it was a time of hope and promise that everything she imagined was possible. Aristotle Onassis, her next husband, was a tycoon whose money could protect and pamper her at a time when her heart was broken and her spirit drained. Maurice Tempelsman, with whom she had a spiritual bond, was a friend and beloved companion. Although they never married, he provided emotional security during the last years of her life, something no man had ever given her before.

More than forty years of Jacqueline Bouvier Kennedy Onassis's life revolved around these three dramatically different men. When she met Jack Kennedy in 1951, she found a man who was perfectly suited to be her husband. The only problem was that he didn't think so. Jack, then thirty-four, was soon to be elected to the U.S. Senate and gave every indication of wanting to remain a perennial bachelor, one not well suited to the role of a married man. His reputation as a womanizer with a perpetually roving eye and a seemingly insatiable appetite for pretty women—especially buxom, blonde babes—could easily have discouraged Jackie or, for that matter, any woman with marriage on her mind.

"I just had the feeling that Jack wasn't ready to get

married," friend and fellow Senator George Smathers remembered. "But I don't know that he would have ever gotten more ready to get married than he was at the time. Look, he was just one of those guys."

Ready or not, Jack was virtually Jackie's psychological twin. As a child of divorce, Jackie was emotionally guarded, while Jack was also distant, having spent much of his childhood sick and alone in a room, away from his cold, seemingly unfeeling mother.

"They had both taken circumstances that weren't the best in the world when they were younger and learned to make themselves up as they went along," said Lem Billings. "They were so much alike. Even the names—Jack and Jackie: two halves of a single whole. They were both actors, and they appreciated each other's performance."

Jackie's mother, Janet Auchincloss, had always urged her daughter to value wealth in a potential mate. After divorcing Jackie's philandering father who had lost much of their money, she married Hugh D. Auchincloss Jr., a well-known name in the Social Register whose family fortune provided a more than comfortable lifestyle for Janet and her two daughters. Jackie, however, found many qualities more appealing about Jack Kennedy than his money. Although she was twelve years younger, Jackie was certain that Jack was destined to be her soul mate, sharing a love of books and history as well as a preference for solitude, away from large parties and meaningless social events. She told a friend, "All I want to do is get married to Jack."

Far from a fairytale courtship, Jack didn't come to Jackie on bended knee and ask for her hand in marriage. She realized that wasn't his style. Like many a woman who wants to marry a man, she recognized that if she wanted to become Mrs. John F. Kennedy, she would have to take charge. While her family's wealth couldn't match that of the Kennedys, she was sure her well-positioned social pedigree, thanks to her Bouvier ancestry and the Auchincloss connection, would be valuable to the striving political aspirations of the Kennedy family and in particular to its patriarch, Joseph Patrick Kennedy, whose own attempts to penetrate high society had been rebuffed at every turn.

Realizing that Joe Kennedy was the key to her campaign, she made him aware of her social connections and what she then believed to be her aristocratic Bouvier background. She also subtly alluded to her impressive educational experiences at Miss Porter's, Vassar, and the Sorbonne and even her Debutante of the Year and Prix de Paris honors. At the same time, Jackie was careful to avoid mentioning her relatively modest financial circumstances of which the elder Kennedy was already aware. And she rarely discussed her less-than-impressive job as Inquiring Photographer for the *Washington Times-Herald*.

Jackie's plan took hold, and within a short time, Joe

Kennedy became her biggest fan. What impressed him most was the trait that Jackie couldn't hide if she had wanted to: her signature, cheeky independence beneath the finishing-school polish. She wasn't afraid to speak her mind around him, and he reveled in it. While Jack and his siblings played touch football on the lawn at the Kennedy compound, Jackie and Joe would sit on the porch, talking about everything from classical music to movies. A few years later, Jackie would say that "next to my husband and my own father, I love Joe Kennedy more than anybody in the world." It didn't take long before Joseph Kennedy not only approved of Jackie, but he was virtually insisting that his son Jack marry her as soon as possible. Still, the prospective groom hesitated. Jack's friend, Lem Billings, once told Kennedy family biographers Peter Collier and David Horowitz that he "couldn't visualize him actually saying 'I love you' to somebody and asking her to marry him. It was the sort of thing he would have liked to have happen without having to talk about it." Jackie had a last-minute opportunity to go to England to cover the coronation of Queen Elizabeth II. Reluctant to be away from Jack, her mother commented, "If you're so much in love with Jack Kennedy that you don't want to leave him, I should think he would be much more likely to find out how he felt about you if you were seeing exciting people and doing exciting things instead of sitting here waiting for the telephone to ring."

Taking her mother's advice to put some distance between

herself and Jack, she left for London. Knowing Jack would see her by-lined articles, Jackie reinforced her absence by sending him letters describing the coronation balls and other parties she was invited to, including the names of some of the eligible men who were escorting her. Within a week, Jack proposed long distance over the telephone.

Jackie, as always, faced the reality of the situation. Although she had finally managed to capture Jack, she knew it was unlikely that he would truly settle down. "How can you live with a husband who is bound to be unfaithful but whom one loves?" she asked a friend. She answered her own question when she recognized that she had always loved rogues, men whose behavior reminded her of her father's. But Jack presented other problems. She wasn't sure if she wanted to be married to a politician, especially to a man who had presidential aspirations. The bonds that united them, however, were too intense to ignore, and on September 12, 1953, she married Jack. Until the time of his assassination ten years later, she loved him for better and for worse until death parted them in November 1963.

The Second Time, Marry for Money

Years later, as the widow whose every move was watched by the entire world, Jackie would find safety and security in Aristotle Onassis, the man who would become her second husband. She and Jack had first met the Greek billionaire in 1956 when they were invited on Onassis's yacht to meet Winston Churchill, Jack's idol. The Kennedys' casual friendship with Onassis continued over the next few years, somewhat strengthened by the romantic relationship Jackie's sister, Lee, had with Onassis. In the summer of 1963, Jackie gave birth prematurely to Patrick Bouvier Kennedy, who lived less than two days. At Lee's suggestion, Onassis offered a Mediterranean cruise on his yacht to help Jackie recover from the depression she suffered after the baby's death. Although Jack was hesitant to have Jackie go, he thought the cruise might be good for her.

Onassis's yacht, the *Christina*, was a massive 303-foot vessel complete with enormous guest suites, movie theater, marble pool, ballroom, library, and sixty servants who catered to a dozen guests. The sea air, the pampering, and the chance to rest from her hectic political schedule lifted her mood, but Jackie's thoughts were mainly of Jack, whom she missed terribly. Each evening she wrote him touching letters, pouring out her heart and speaking of her tremendous love for him. "I loved you from the moment I saw you," she wrote, while adding how much she depended on him and how worried she was about the stress his job created. The cruise revived Jackie's sagging spirits, and she was also favorably impressed with Onassis, remarking that he was "an alive and vital person who had come from nowhere" to become a stunning success. As much

as she had enjoyed herself, she was eager to return to her husband and children.

The serenity Jackie felt while at sea was soon to be destroyed
by an assassin's bullet. Onassis was among the many who
called on Jackie at the White House to pay his respects. Widowed at age thirty-four, Jackie withdrew from public life.
Eventually she began seeing friends again, and Onassis was
among them. Given the disparity of their backgrounds, no one
assumed there was any romantic involvement. However, their
friendship deepened and, in 1968, reached a level where they
considered marriage, alarming the Kennedy family, who felt
Jackie's relationship with Onassis could harm Bobby Kennedy's candidacy for the presidency. Jackie, however, would not
be discouraged. In May of that year, she introduced Onassis to
her mother and stepfather as a prospective spouse.

A month later, Jackie's greatest fear was realized—another
Kennedy was murdered. Bobby Kennedy's death shattered
Jackie, and she was frightened for her own life and particularly
for the safety of her children, believing that all Kennedys were
targets for murder. In a state of panic, she blurted, "I hate this
country. I despise America, and I don't want my children to
live here any more. If they are killing Kennedys, my kids are
number-one targets . . . I want to get out of this country."
Deeply in shock and wanting comfort and security, she decided
to accept Onassis's proposal of marriage.

When told by a friend that if she married Onassis it would probably remove her from the pedestal she had been placed upon following her husband's death, Jackie replied, "That's better than freezing there." The decision to marry Onassis was not a popular one, and millions of admirers expressed their displeasure. However, Jackie recognized what she needed at this point in her life, and she married Onassis in October 1968.

As a potential husband for Jackie, Onassis would not seem to be a natural choice for the tall, beautiful, young widow. At five feet, five inches tall, he was almost two inches shorter than Jackie. Although he was twenty-three years older, his swarthy, weathered looks made him seem even more so. A self-made man, he had earned his fortune in shipping, estimated at more than $300 million by 1960, which is more than a billion and a half in today's dollars.

Onassis not only offered financial and physical security, he was also anxious to please Jackie, seeing her as a prized jewel. He showered her with attention, offered her comfort and understanding, and was especially attentive to her children, Caroline and John.

Much like her father, Onassis was somewhat of a bad boy, and Jackie responded to this aspect of his personality. She was attracted to his earthy sensuality, and he managed to break through her reserve into her more uninhibited side. Somewhat dramatically, Onassis compared Jackie to a diamond, "Cool and sharp at the edges, fiery and hot beneath the surface."

Over time the relationship soured, particularly following the death of his son and his own declining health. Onassis had started divorce proceedings when he died in 1975. Despite the many times he had chosen to make disparaging comments publicly about Jackie, she refrained from saying anything negative about his behavior.

After the funeral, Jackie released this statement to the press: "Aristotle Onassis rescued me at a moment when my life was engulfed with shadows. He meant a lot to me. He brought me into a world where one could find both happiness and love. We lived through many beautiful experiences together which cannot be forgotten and for which I will be eternally grateful."

As always, Jackie was gracious and eloquent in her farewell to Onassis. While she was careful not to say that she loved him or even that he would be missed, it was obvious that she appreciated their happy days together.

Following his death, Jackie again surprised the world with her decision to become a working woman—taking a position at a New York publishing house as a consulting editor. "I have always lived through men; now I realize I can't do that anymore," she said. As one of America's fifty wealthiest women, she was financially independent and her choice to work was based on doing something she enjoyed, as well as utilizing her education and experiences. What were well-educated women supposed to do when the children were grown, she once asked, "Watch the raindrops coming down the windowpane?"

The Third Time, Marry for Companionship

In her choice of the next man in her life, Maurice Tempelsman, Jackie was perhaps subconsciously following her own advice that a woman's third partner should be for companionship. It was in the early 1980s that she formed a close relationship with Tempelsman, the son of Orthodox Jews. Tempelsman, whom she had met years earlier when Jack was still alive, was a successful financier and diamond merchant as well as a major contributor to the Democratic Party. He became her financial adviser when Onassis died and is reputed to have quadrupled her $26 million inheritance.

Tempelsman, who offered far more than financial acumen, was extremely attentive to Jackie and, in 1982, moved into her Fifth Avenue apartment. In looks and temperament, Tempelsman was unlike any other man Jackie had been closely involved with. Lacking the handsome face and physique of John Kennedy and the billions of Onassis, he more than made up for it with his keen intellect, sharp wit, and respect for learning. Unlike her husbands, she was his main focus, not his work or other women. Spending most of their time with each other, he was her constant companion. They shared vacations, read poetry together, took walks in the park, and celebrated major holidays with her daughter, Caroline, and her son-in-law, Ed Schlossberg, along with Jackie's three grandchildren. Her beloved son, John, often joined them as well.

Maurice, never too busy for Jackie, even took the time to go with her when she picked up a newspaper at the nearby stationers. According to Jimmy Ezra, "Jackie was my customer since I opened the store in the mid-'70s. I first met her when she was married to Onassis. After he died, she often came into the store with Maurice to pick up fashion magazines like *Vogue* or *W*, which she particularly liked to read. Jackie and Maurice were like two children together, laughing and joking. In the almost twenty years that I knew her, Jackie never seemed happier."

From 1975 until 1994, the year of her death, Jackie was extremely fulfilled both personally and professionally. In Maurice, she had finally found a man who was more interested in pleasing her than the reverse. While this period of unbroken happiness appeared as if it would endure for many years, it was not Jackie's fate to grow old together with Maurice. In early 1994, discovering that she had non-Hodgkin's lymphoma, Jackie began a program of aggressive chemotherapy. Continually by her side, Maurice accompanied her to these treatments, took her for walks in the park, bought her favorite flowers every day, and, at the end, was at her bedside, kissing her forehead as she lapsed into a final sleep. She died on May 19, 1994. Literally with her in sickness and in health, Maurice was there for Jackie at the most critical time of her life.

Jack and Jackie

Jackie was buried next to her husband, Jack Kennedy, at Arlington National Cemetery, the place where her family and America wanted her to be. United in death, as they had been in life, Jack and Jackie will always be America's most luminous couple, romanticized and revered, who engaged our hearts and imagination like never before or since.

"For one brief shining moment, there was Camelot."

What Jackie Taught Us

Jacqueline Kennedy Onassis was legendary for her ability to captivate some of the most interesting men of the twentieth century. To the casual observer, this might be puzzling, because Jackie didn't project an image of breathtaking beauty, an outgoing personality, or some form of primal sexuality. What was it about Jackie then that resulted in such adoration from the opposite sex? The answer is simple yet difficult, subtle yet obvious, unique yet universal.

Jackie taught us that the most intriguing asset every woman possesses is her own individuality. In a world dominated by provocative advertising, reinforced by an entertainment culture that projects perfect bodies, daring fashion, and overt sexuality, it's easy to reject one's essential self. When we recast ourselves in a weak imitation of an image that has been presented by others, we mute our own essence, our strongest suit.

There is a distinct difference, however, between simply being one's self and being the best we can be. As a young woman, Jackie was brutally honest with herself and set out to improve what she believed to be her shortcomings. There was a litany of things she wanted to fix, whether it was her hands and feet that her mother told her were unattractively large, her hair that she found perpetually unmanageable, or her hips that she felt were too wide. Determined to learn how to mask her physical imperfections, she scrutinized fashion magazines and consulted with hair and beauty experts. Rather than allowing herself to feel rejected, she made the most of what she had. In tallying her strong suits, Jackie recognized that she was well educated, well read, and had a keen intellect. She understood that her international travels had given her a patina of sophistication that not every woman could claim. Although as a young woman she didn't have a large clothing budget, Jackie was grateful she had inherited the good taste of both her parents, who had instilled in her the importance of an attractive appearance. Men found all these attributes extremely desirable, and it gave Jackie an edge. It made her more than just another pretty face.

Eager to improve herself, Jackie was always open to helpful advice from people she trusted. Black Jack, her flamboyant father, was one of them. We can benefit from a number of techniques he taught Jackie that would work for any woman. It was from her father that she learned to make the object of her attention the center of the universe at that particular moment. She perfected the "lighthouse look," locking eyes with a man, beaming at him with great intensity, and seemingly ignoring everything and everyone else. Jackie's father encouraged her to take advantage of a radiant smile and an uplifted chin and to maintain a restrained demeanor to convey a sense of elusiveness. His advice also emphasized the merits of speaking softly and never revealing everything.

Jackie was adept at transferring the same techniques that attracted men in her romantic relationships to other areas of her life. She had no hesitation about using her wonderful smile and infectious charm on an ambassador, an eminent judge, or a waiter. She refused to be cowed by men whom others found intimidating and almost always won them over by her intelligence and empathy. They were all unaware that she was using her father's favorite technique—"the lighthouse look"—on them.

Men never found Jackie to be a clinging vine. She was a very independent person with a range of interests that didn't necessarily include them. Men were not only fascinated by her, they were never bored. And because she was her own person, they never felt drained by her.

Jackie also taught us that sometimes it's impossible to avoid heartache, unhappiness, and even failure with those we love.

She may have consulted her head, but she always followed her heart. Each of her relationships with men to whom she was committed brought her happiness, albeit each of a different nature. Ultimately, she could look back and know that she had experienced the exhilaration of true love with Jack Kennedy, that she had tasted the passionate excitement of a relationship with a "forbidden" man in Aristotle Onassis, and that she had been blessed in her later years with the loyalty and affection of a close companion in Maurice Tempelsman.

What we learn from Jackie is that there is no perfect man or marriage. There are always compromises. It's up to each of us to determine if the good outweighs the bad. Love and marriage are never easy, but Jackie's life demonstrates that making the commitment is always worth the risk.

An Innate Wisdom

A. E. Hotchner is the author of *Papa Hemingway* and *O.J. in the Morning, G&T at Night*.

ON JANUARY 13, 1961, I was visiting my longtime friend Ernest Hemingway in his secured room in the psychiatric section of St. Mary's Hospital in Rochester, Minnesota, when he received a telegram from president-elect Kennedy, inviting Ernest and his wife, Mary, to be his personal guests at the impending inaugural.

When I came into his room that morning, he was unsuccessfully trying to write the final chapter of his Paris memoir, a loving tribute to his first wife, Hadley. He asked me to help him compose a reply to Kennedy's invitation. It took a while, but eventually we produced a graceful declination, which I telegraphed to the White House when I returned to my hotel.

Ernest told me he was truly sorry not to be able to be at the inauguration, that he admired the young couple and thought that they would be a good tonic for the country and freshen up the bad taste of current politics. He said he had been following Kennedy's progress and likened Jackie's devotion and support to what Hadley had given him as a young, struggling writer in Paris. He said that the two toughest jobs of wife-ing are being married to a struggling politician or to a writer. He said he hoped Kennedy would not follow his own bad example, that he would keep Jackie and her demonstrated virtues solidly at his side.

In the fourteen years of our shared exploits and adventures, Ernest often referred to his early days in Paris with his newly wedded bride. She was the first love of his life, but young as he was, how could he know that that first love would be the only true love of his life? Hadley also came to realize that she should not have departed so soon, that she should have weathered the storm and preserved the good of what they had.

From the moment Jackie fell in love with Kennedy, her first love, it was a love that never wavered. She knew from the start that she was in a very green pasture—greener than any that may be beyond.

Jackie's strength was in sensing from the very beginning the vitality and joy of their being committed to each other, an innate wisdom that served her very well as wife, mother, and First Lady.

That Rarest of Gems

Malachy McCourt is an actor, activist, columnist, and
author of *Malachy McCourt's History of Ireland*, *A Monk
Swimming*, and other works.

Rose Kennedy once said, "I've had an exciting time; I
married for love and got a little money along with it." So
I wonder if Jackie didn't want to impress her mother-in-law
when she was reported to have opined, "The first time you
marry for love, the second for money, and the third for companionship."

An astonishingly beautiful woman, Jackie outshone all
those around her. She was a woman who loved and won and
who certainly had loved and lost.

Although twice married and in other serious relationships—
and a mother a couple of times over—Jackie Kennedy carried
an air of virginal innocence about her for her entire life. Perhaps this well-honed image was encouraged by her father,
Black Jack Bouvier, who, by example, taught her the art of

seduction without having to go all the way, as it was termed in those days.

The Kennedy males, like all good Irish Catholics, were puritanical when it came to the womenfolk. She was a devoted wife to John F. Kennedy and sacrificed much to become a magnificent First Lady. In her earliest days in the White House, she declared, "I'll be a wife and mother first, then First Lady." Yet she was as married to America as she was to him. She used the charismatic power of her charm not only on the men in her life but to gain new respect worldwide for these United States.

She may have been a romantic in her tastes but was decidedly pragmatic when it came to marriage: She is reported to have said, "I do not think that there are any men who are faithful to their wives."

And did she love Aristotle Onassis? Does it matter now? From all the accounts, I think Jackie did love Onassis—particularly in the beginning, before his son died and his health and financial empire declined. He was charming, intelligent, and coddled her—yes, with jewels, but also with protection.

If someone is going to provide you and your children with everything that you need in this life there is hardly any reason not to love him *and* like him. In her own determined way she defied the expectations of family, friends, and the public with her decision to marry him because her first priority was the safety and security of her children.

Jackie possessed an air of saintliness—some might say coolness—that would not allow any of us ordinary punters to even think of asking her for a date. She did see my friend the writer Pete Hamill for a time. Gentleman that he is, his lips have remained glued as to how intimate that relationship was. Did he make love to her? If he said yes, who would believe him? If he said no, the crude ones would ask, What was the point of dating her? You can't win.

In her last years, it was with "savvy, cultivated Maurice Tempelsman [that] Jacqueline Kennedy Onassis at long last found a safe haven—and serenity." She was good to her word and "seemed to have found that rarest of gems: a genuine soul mate"—and a true companion.

Reading these reflections published in *People* magazine shortly after her death, calls to mind the lines from W. B. Yeats's "When You Are Old":

How many loved your moments of glad grace,
And loved your beauty with love false or true,
But one man loved the pilgrim soul in you,
And loved the sorrows of your changing face . . .

I too shared a love of her "pilgrim soul," albeit like so many, from afar.

"I knew right away that Jackie was different from all the other girls Jack had been dating. She was more intelligent, more literary, more substantial. . . . They were kindred souls. Jack and Jackie, two halves of the same whole."

—LEMOYNE BILLINGS

What Jackie Taught Us About
Motherhood

PROVIDING LOVE, SECURITY, AND
DISCIPLINE WITHOUT TEARS

"All that I am or ever hope to be, I owe to my angel Mother."
—Abraham Lincoln (1809–1865)

THE MEMORY OF our mother never leaves us—the good, the bad, and the ugly. That Jackie Kennedy Onassis was an exceptionally good mother even her harshest detractors readily acknowledge. Motherhood was what mattered most to Jackie. She believed that absolutely nothing came before the welfare of her children. Indeed, she referred to her efforts in raising Caroline and John Jr. as the best thing she'd ever done, saying she wanted to be remembered for that achievement more than for any other. She once remarked, "If you bungle raising your children, I don't think whatever else you do well matters very much."

When Caroline Bouvier Kennedy was born on November

27, 1957, Jackie was heartened to see how quickly Jack became a warm, loving father to his daughter. "That was a marvelous relationship," recalled family friend Betty Spaulding. "Until he had Caroline, he never really learned how to deal with people. It was fascinating to watch him grow in this capacity."

Seeing her emotionally reserved husband be so responsive to Caroline must have brought a sense of relief to Jackie. Growing up as the son of a philandering father and a distant, obsessively religious mother, Jack seemed wary of intimate, emotional relationships, despite an outwardly gregarious manner. "My mother was either at some Paris fashion house or else on her knees in some church," Jack once bitterly told a friend. "She was never here when we really needed her. . . . My mother never really held me and hugged me. Never! Never!"

Coming from a broken home, Jackie's own childhood carried a different kind of baggage. Her philandering father, John "Black Jack" Vernou Bouvier III, and unhappy mother, Janet Lee Bouvier, were constantly battling. Their eventual divorce when Jackie was eleven created a sense of isolation and emotional reserve that never left her. Janet and Jack were polar opposites on the parenting scale. Her father indulged Jackie's every whim, while her mother was critical and demanding. Although Janet diligently looked after Jackie's every need, her relentless focus on perfection left little room for warmth or affection. It was her father who poured out the unconditional love that gave Jackie the self-confidence and sense of worth that is so important to all of us. Acknowledging that her mother had tried to do her best, Jackie especially appreciated Janet's efforts to nurture her creative instincts while encouraging her to be the best in everything she undertook. "I hope I do as well for my children as my mother did for me," she once said.

"Trust Your Instincts"

Putting aside the sadness and insecurity she had experienced as a child, Jackie was determined to be the best possible mother for her own children. "People have too many theories about rearing children," she said. "I believe simply in love, security, and discipline." She constantly read books on child psychology but frequently turned to the practical wisdom of the renowned childrearing expert of the 1960s—Dr. Benjamin Spock, pediatrician and best-selling author. His advice to new parents to "trust your instincts . . . you know more than you think you do" must have been a comforting thought to Jackie as a first-time mother at age twenty-eight.

"I always imagined I'd raise my children completely on my own," said Jackie. "But once you have them, you find you need help. So I do need Dr. Spock a lot, and I find it such a relief to know that other people's children are as bad as yours at the same age." Years later, her well-worn copy of his book, *Dr. Spock's Baby and Child Care*, would fetch $6,900 at the famed Sotheby's Jackie Kennedy Onassis estate sale.

Having a full-time nanny was an accepted custom in Jackie's family and, as the wife of a busy senator who would soon become president, it was an obvious necessity in Jackie's mind. She admired the dedicated manner in which the English brought up their children, and shortly before Caroline's birth Jackie chose Maud Shaw, a middle-aged English woman, to be the nanny for her children. Nanny Shaw, who would stay with the Kennedy family for seven and a half years, supervised the children on a day-to-day basis according to Jackie's direction.

Jackie's approach to mothering was completely compatible with Ms. Shaw's view on being a good nanny: love, a sense of fair play, the ability to discipline without tears, and the understanding that each child is different and should be handled and treated differently. Shaw was invaluable to Jackie, who, with her myriad duties as First Lady, was a de facto working woman. However, Jackie was never too busy for her children and willingly rearranged her schedule so she could be with them.

She once said, "I think it's hard enough to bring up children anyway, and everyone knows that limelight is the worst thing for them. They either get conceited or else they get hurt. . . . They need their mother's affection and guidance and long periods of time alone with her. That is what gives them security in an often confusing new world."

Although the term *quality time* wasn't used during the 1960s, Jackie knew the importance of spending uninterrupted periods every day with her children that allowed her to be completely focused and involved. She put her role as a mother before her job as First Lady, even refusing to perform many of the duties generally expected of her, such as meeting and greeting representatives of various groups and dignitaries visiting the White House. Instead, she would relegate the chore to the vice president's wife, Lady Bird Johnson, or even to Rose Kennedy, her mother-in-law.

"I watched her in the White House doggedly keep a lot of time for the children," recalled Tish Baldrige. "It was difficult to do, but she did it. She simply changed her schedule."

Within a short time, Jackie was able to assert herself as a confident mother who answered to no one, including her opinionated mother-in-law, when it came to her children. As the mother of nine, Rose Kennedy regarded herself as the ultimate matriarch and child-rearing authority and did not hesitate to offer her unsolicited advice, even going so far as to mail reminders to Jackie to make sure that the children drank their milk and went to Mass.

When visiting her son Jack's Georgetown house one day, Rose thought that Caroline should not be outside playing because she was going to have her photograph taken later that day. She was about to tell Caroline to go indoors, when, without hesitation, Jackie told Rose not to interfere, that Caroline should be able to run and play outdoors like any normal child. "The difference between us," she told her mother-in-law, "is that you want Caroline to grow up to be like you, and I want her to grow up and be like me."

Battling for Privacy

By the time John Fitzgerald Kennedy Jr. was born on November 25, 1960, press mania was at a fever pitch because the baby's father was the newly elected president. Jackie now had to face the special problems of bringing up her children in the White House. She worried about the effect of never-ending public and press attention, which she believed would deprive them of their childhood and prevent them from leading normal lives.

Jackie immediately began a never-ending battle for her children's privacy and soon found herself constantly at war with White House Press Secretary Pierre Salinger. Once, after Jack had conspired with Salinger to have the children photographed when she was away, Jackie wrote a stern memo to Salinger, saying, "I want no more—I mean this—and if you are firm and will take the time, you can stop it. So please do. What is a press secretary for—to help with the press, yes—but also to protect us?" Salinger explained that, "Jackie was just ferociously protective of their privacy. From the moment she set foot in the White House, she wanted to keep them out of the spotlight."

To prevent the curiosity-seekers and tourists from gawking at her and the children, Jackie decided to enlist the aid of the

White House gardeners, directing them to "grow rhododendrons sky-high" and plant trees and shrubs at strategic points to block their view. At first, Jack protested, reminding her that the White House is public property and that people have a right to look at it. Jackie agreed but added, "They're entitled to some view of the White House. . . . But I'm sick and tired of starring in everyone's home movies!" White House usher J. B. West once commented that if Jackie were in charge, "The White House would be surrounded by high brick walls. And a moat with crocodiles."

Unlike Jackie, Jack Kennedy's family thought that putting the children in the spotlight was completely harmless and, undoubtedly, would help their father's political career. Jackie took great exception to this and at times even had to battle her husband as to when and if the children could be photographed.

She refused to allow any unplanned or unapproved photographs either of her children or herself. Eventually, she permitted *Look* and *Life* magazines to photograph Caroline and John as long as it was scheduled ahead of time and under her control. Some of the most famous images taken included the children in Halloween costumes, Caroline riding her pony, and little John and his sister dancing a jig in the Oval Office while their father clapped. They became classic, beloved pictures of America's First Family.

Raising Children in the White House

Jackie was also adamant that the children not have the sense of living in formal staterooms, surrounded by Secret Service agents and presidential staffers. She believed that it was important to create a warm and comfortable environment that would counteract the grandeur and formality of the White House. When they moved in, Jackie's first priority was to redecorate the children's rooms, transforming the "hotel décor" that had been put in place by the Eisenhowers to something far more appealing. Caroline's room was in a feminine pink and white, complete with a canopy bed, rocking horse, and a Grandma Moses painting on the wall. Baby John's room was painted white, accented by blue crown molding. Between the children's rooms, Maud Shaw was housed in a small room. In complimenting Jackie's efforts, Tish Baldrige said, "She turned this drafty, cold old place into a warm environment for a young family overnight."

When media attention and security concerns made it difficult for Caroline to attend her Georgetown playgroup, Jackie decided that she would create a play-schoolroom at the White House. She designed the room, complete with rabbit cages, guinea pigs, goldfish, plants, blackboards, dress-up clothes, and sand tables, and stocked it with hundreds of schoolbooks from a list she acquired from a preschool teacher.

Even after the school was in full swing with ten little boys and girls attending, Jackie continued to think of unique ways to supplement the curriculum with special events for the children. Once, she arranged for a delegation of Native Americans, who had come to the White House in full regalia, to visit the classroom and lead the children in a spirited rain dance.

Jackie believed that nothing was more important for her children than the joy of exuberant play and created an elaborate play area for Caroline and John and their friends. Nearly hidden under the trees near the West Wing, this wonderful playground was built by White House carpenters according to Jackie's carefully drawn sketches. There was a leather swing, a slide, a barrel tunnel, a trampoline, a rabbit hutch, and a tree house with a slide mounted inside the branches of former President Herbert Hoover's white oak tree.

Jackie heartily endorsed the philosophy of child-rearing experts who advocated having animals in the household to help children develop self-confidence, empathy, and responsibility in addition to providing companionship. Jackie had fond memories of growing up with a white rabbit, Bull Terrier, Dachshund, Dalmatian, and her own first dog, a Scottish Terrier named Hootchie. Deciding it was important for Caroline and John to have the same experience, Jackie finally convinced her husband that their children shouldn't be deprived of a simple pleasure that most children were able to enjoy, despite living in the White House and Jack's allergies.

As the children grew, so did their menagerie of pets. Jackie had the carpenters build doghouses for Charlie and Pushinka;

a stable for horses Macaroni and Tex; and pens for the lambs, ducks, and guinea pigs. Caroline's hamsters, Marybell and Bluebell, and Robin, the canary, remained in her bedroom.

Years later, John Kennedy Jr. reminisced about one of their dogs. "We had a dog who was named Pushinka," said John, "who was given to my father by the premier of Russia, the Soviet Union at that time. . . . It was the daughter of the first dog in space. And we trained it to slide down this slide that we had in the back of the White House. Sliding the dog down the slide is probably my first memory."

Proper Names and Courtesies

Jackie believed it was essential that her children learn proper manners and to show respect for others, and she taught Caroline and John not only basic table manners and courtesies but also to be considerate of others by working on their relationships with visitors and White House employees. Leaving nothing to chance, Jackie made sure they learned to properly greet people by saying, "How do you do?" not only to friends of their parents but also to the butlers, maids, police officers, ushers, Secret Service agents, kitchen and pantry staff, gardeners, and whomever else they passed. All adults, from White House maids to cabinet members, were addressed as Mr., Mrs., or Miss. "The children were well-behaved because their mother would not have it any other way," said Tish Baldrige.

It was a White House tradition for heads of state to visit the family quarters to have a cocktail with President and Mrs. Kennedy before meeting with the guests for state dinners in their honor. Tish Baldrige recalled, "Caroline and John, usually in their pajamas and robes, were always brought in to meet the guests of honor on these occasions. They were taught how to shake hands, as part of the meeting ritual. Sometimes John would bow and Caroline would curtsy."

With her love of history that she wanted to pass on to her children, Jackie would take the time to tell Caroline and John about the customs and traditions of a country if they were receiving important foreign visitors, as when the Shah of Iran was in town. "You'll see the Shah of Iran tonight, who lives far, far away in Persia," Jackie said to the children. "He has two little children your ages. They live in a palace. His wife, called an empress, like in the storybooks, is very beautiful, and they have asked particularly to meet the two of you, so they can return home and tell their own children about you."

Early on, Jackie taught them the importance of giving and receiving gifts by including them in a White House tradition where there was an exchange of gifts between the heads of state during the cocktail hour upstairs before the state dinner began on the lower floor. Whenever the visitors had children, Caroline and John would offer to the visitors beautifully wrapped presents that had the names of their children on the gift cards. Then they would unwrap the gifts from the children of the visitors.

Knowing how strongly children respond to visual and aural stimulation, Jackie made it a point to take Caroline and John down to the South Lawn to watch the military salute given to visiting heads of state. There they could see the colorful ceremonies of marching bands, waving flags, the review of the troops, and the booming firing of cannons.

Encouraging Creativity

A passionate believer in the arts, Jackie was eager to nurture creativity in her children, something her mother had done for her as a child. "My mother helped us enormously with our creative instincts," said Jackie. "She interested us in languages, poetry, and art as young children. She encouraged us to make things for birthday presents instead of buying them. So perhaps we would paint a picture or write a poem or memorize something." Jackie passed this same philosophy on to Caroline and urged her daughter to try her hand at writing poetry, something her Grandfather Bouvier had also encouraged her to do as a child. When Caroline was fourteen, she composed a special poem for her grandmother, Rose Kennedy, about her brother John:

He comes spitting in my room, jabbing left and right
Shouting, OK, Caroline, ready for a fight?
He is trying to blow us up with his chemistry set,
He has killed all the plants but we've escaped as yet,

He loves my mother's linen sheets and hates his own percale.
He can imitate the sounds of a humpback whale.
I love him not because I oughter
But also because blood runs thicker than water.

Painting was a lifelong hobby for Jackie, and whenever she set up her materials to paint, she put up a child's paint box beside her for five-year-old Caroline as a first step in developing her creativity. "She really prefers to dip the brushes in water, smear the paints, and make a mess," said Jackie, "but it is a treat for her to paint with her mother. Perhaps this will develop a latent talent; perhaps it will merely do what it did for me, produce occasional paintings which only one's family could admire, and be a source of pleasure and relaxation."

Jackie enlisted Nanny Shaw's help in developing the children's concentration skills. Ms. Shaw would sit Caroline down with a drawing book and crayons and encourage her to draw, suggesting things she might like to sketch. John would have a pile of colored bricks, and she would help him start to balance the bricks on top of each other. "I have found that you have to teach children concentration; it is not something they are born with," said Ms. Shaw. "They gradually become interested in doing it for themselves, and they will unconsciously learn to concentrate."

Good, Clean Fun

An essential ingredient for children, Jackie believed, is having simple fun, and she went to great lengths to make sure that Caroline and John did not miss out on the ordinary pleasures and adventures of childhood, despite having such a high public profile. Jackie frequently would don a wig and disguise herself so she could take them to amusement parks, movies, and picnics without being noticed by the press.

Arthur Schlesinger Jr., a journalist who wrote about the Washington political scene, recalled Halloween evening 1962, when his fourteen-year-old daughter Christina opened their front door to a group of tiny, costumed trick-or-treaters, including one who was especially eager to have her basket filled. Christina would not have recognized the little girl until she heard the mother, wearing a mask and standing in the background, say that it was time to go. The voice was unmistakably that of Jackie, who was taking Caroline and her little cousins through the neighborhood. In late 1960, Jackie convinced Jack to lease Glen Ora, a country house in Middleburg, Virginia, where they would regularly spend weekends and vacations. She wanted Caroline and John Jr. to have the normalcy of being able to run and play in relative privacy. Glen Ora was a four hundred–acre estate with a French-style country manor house, guest cottages, swimming pool, and stables. Nestled deep in the countryside with lots of green pastures, streams and springs, wild turkeys, and horses, it was a peaceful haven for the family. Often she and the children would spend four days a week there, with Jack joining them on weekends. Later, they would build Wexford, intended to be their own retreat in Virginia.

On their long weekends at Glen Ora, social life centered on her children, and only four times in the two years that they leased the house did Jackie even go out to eat—twice at a restaurant and twice at friends' homes. She referred to Glen Ora as "home" and delighted in quiet, simple pleasures like changing diapers, bathing John and Caroline, and reading them to sleep. It was here that Jackie, who counted horseback riding among her greatest pastimes, began teaching four-year-old Caroline to ride and care for horses.

After Jack had completed two years in office, Jackie was asked what she hoped to accomplish during the remaining two. "More time with my children," she said, "for they are both at an age where it is important that their parents be with them as much as possible." True to her word, Jackie cut back even more from her White House duties.

A Single Mother

The assassination of President John Kennedy in November 1963 was a horrific blow to the country and a devastating loss to his wife and children. During his funeral, Jackie did not try to shield Caroline and John from the somber ceremonies and glare of publicity, instinctively realizing that it was important for them and for the country that they be together throughout this ordeal. She even managed to celebrate John's third birthday on the night of her husband's burial by going ahead with his party and then again for Caroline's birthday two days later.

As a widow with two children, Jackie faced all the challenges of a single mother, with the additional burden of having an entire world watching to see how she would manage on her own. On a visit to Press Secretary Pierre Salinger's office during the weekend following the funeral, Jackie said, "Pierre, I have nothing else to do in life now except to raise my children well, to help them move forward through this terrible thing—otherwise, they will be tied forever to their father's death. I have to make sure they survive." Within a few months, she and the children left Washington, DC, and moved to New York City to start a new life.

A New Life in New York

Jackie did all the things most mothers do: She walked her children to school, took them for carousel rides in Central Park, attended their plays and recitals, brought them to the beach, and took them on skiing trips. However, the children missed their father terribly, and young John, eager for a father figure, tended to gravitate to various men in the Kennedy employ.

As a small child, John asked a Secret Service agent if he was a daddy. Acknowledging that he was, John asked poignantly, "Then will you throw me up in the air?"

Dr. Spock's advice that "everybody knows that children are born with quite different temperaments" must have reassured Jackie as she was faced with two completely different children to raise. Caroline, who looked like her father but was in lockstep with Jackie's approach to life, was shy and reserved. She was also studious and respectful of the wishes of her elders. Jackie's handsome, dark-haired son, on the other hand, looked like a Bouvier but behaved like a Kennedy. A complete extrovert and a real daredevil, he got into fistfights with school chums at Collegiate and continually struggled with his studies, much to Jackie's chagrin. While always a sweet-natured child who tried very hard to please his mother, John, particularly as a young adult, preferred a more unconventional lifestyle, which worried Jackie, especially when he told her he thought he might want to be an actor. His flying lessons particularly distressed her, as Jack's sister, Kathleen, as well as his brother Joe had died in plane crashes. His brother Teddy narrowly escaped death in another air collision.

Jackie accepted and nurtured the differences in both her daughter and son, with the result that neither child ever felt jealous or inferior to the other. Instead, there was a deep and abiding love between them. Her son once commented, "My mother has never had an agenda for me or my sister. That's probably why we're all so close and have had a relatively normal life."

As the children of famous parents, Caroline and John were often treated differently by the parents of their friends. Once when Caroline was not invited to another girl's birthday party, Jackie telephoned one of the mothers to ask why. "Of course, we'd love to invite Caroline," the woman stammered, "but we all felt it might be presumptuous of us to ask." Jackie replied, "Please invite Caroline to everything! She's dying to come." Caroline was soon the most popular student at school.

Jackie's brother-in-law Robert Kennedy was a devoted surrogate father to Caroline and John. Following the assassination of her husband, Jackie had come to rely on Bobby for support. He provided solace and strength to her and usually was the first person she turned to for help and advice. However, the Kennedys and Jackie didn't always see eye-to-eye, and money was frequently at the heart of it. While they could easily justify spending millions on politics, when it came to the necessities of everyday life, they could be more than penurious. There are legendary stories about Joe and Rose's cost-consicous ways, including painting only the front of their Palm Beach home because the back would not be seen by passersby.

Jackie was greatly dependent on the Kennedys for financial support, as most of Jack's money was held in trust for their children and she lived off the interest as well as a small widow's pension. Even when she needed to purchase a new car, Jackie had to justify the expenditure and explain why she couldn't continue to drive the old one.

Financial Independence at What Price

When Jackie married Greek billionaire Aristotle Onassis in 1968, the financial independence she wanted for herself and her children was finally possible. Even though Onassis's primary residence was Greece, Jackie wanted to spend as much time as possible with Caroline and John. Prior to their marriage, Jackie made an agreement with Onassis that she would spend the school year with her children in New York City. Although Jackie enjoyed Onassis's company, he, unlike her, was a notorious night owl. She routinely did not accompany him to nightclubs when he came to New York but instead would have an early dinner and go to bed so she could get up with Caroline and John in the morning before they left for school.

An extremely protective mother, Jackie always had her children's welfare in mind. Fritz Selby remembers, "I ran into her at a dinner party in Manhattan and mentioned that I was taking my son, Christopher, who was a student at St. David's with her son John, to a movie the next day. She asked if John could possibly go, too. Of course, I said yes. The next day my son and I picked John up at her apartment at 1040 Fifth Avenue. When we were leaving, Jackie looked me directly in the eye and said, 'Please don't let him cross the street unless he's holding your hand.'"

Always wanting to be part of their world, Jackie encouraged her children to share with her the books and magazines they read and to play the pop music they liked. When she worried that they watched too much television, Jackie invented games to interest them in geography, history, and literature, much as her mother and grandfather had done for her.

After the death of Onassis, Jackie went to work in the publishing world but specified that she would be in the office only three days a week, enabling her to devote the majority of her time to her children.

When the school year finished, Jackie, always imaginative, made sure that summers and other school vacations were special times for Caroline and John. When they were younger, they enjoyed playing with their cousins at Hyannisport; skiing in Colorado, Vermont, and Switzerland; and visiting their grandmother at Newport.

Summers Full of Challenge

As they grew older, Jackie took steps to see that, instead of becoming spoiled, rich kids with too much time on their hands, Caroline and John undertook challenging, enriching activities during the summer either doing volunteer work, taking art-study courses, or, in her son's case, engaging in supervised outdoor activities.

Caroline worked in her Uncle Ted Kennedy's Washington

office and later helped to make a documentary film on coal-miners' families in the Appalachian region. She also was an intern at the *New York Daily News*. After graduation from Concord Academy, she deferred her studies at Harvard's Radcliffe College to enroll in Sotheby's ten-month "Works of Art" course in London. Jackie wholeheartedly approved of this choice, telling a friend that "One day Caroline will have money and she will be better off for having the taste not to waste it."

John's summers were filled with adventure, as Jackie wanted to encourage the maturity and toughness that she knew he would need as an adult. At her instigation, John participated in an Outward Bound course in Maine, went on a diving expedition for buried treasure on a pirate ship off Cape Cod, was a low-paid wrangler at a cattle ranch, and also spent ten weeks in Kenya as part of a survival course. Jackie made sure that he was aware of the needs of those less fortunate and set up volunteer work for him teaching English to immigrants, serving as an intern at the Center for Democratic Policy, and helping as a Peace Corps volunteer to rebuild the town of Rabinal, Guatemala, following a devastating earthquake.

When Caroline and John became young adults, Jackie was anxious that they limit the time spent with Ethel Kennedy's children, some of whom were increasingly spinning out of control after their father, Robert, died. At Hyannisport, there were reports that some of them tossed lit firecrackers into homes, vandalized boats, and fired BB guns. Later on, there were arrests for marijuana possession, then reports of heroin use. Not wanting her children to be exposed to this, Jackie bought land and built her own home on Martha's Vineyard, where Caroline and John could enjoy their summers. Still wanting to maintain contact with her in-laws, once a year she would host a party there for the Kennedy clan.

Her Two Miracles

Jackie was a contemporary, forward-thinking woman, but she had many traditional, old-fashioned values that she passed on to her children. Although Jackie had to be both mother and father to her children, she was no pushover. Strict but loving, she kept a vigilant eye on their activities, and it was obvious that they knew it. Throughout her life, she tried to show Caroline and John by her own example how to be independent, responsible, and thoughtful. As proof that she succeeded, Senator Edward Kennedy affectionately remarked at her funeral, "Her two children turned out to be extraordinary, honest, unspoiled, and with a character equal to hers. And she did it in the most trying of circumstances. They are her two miracles."

Mrs. Kennedy Would Never Let Caroline Do That!

Marguerite Kelly is a syndicated columnist and coauthor of *The Mother's Almanac*.

JACK KENNEDY RAN the country in the early 1960s, but it was Jackie who ran the White House—and our house and probably half the houses in America. She was "the Presence" that young mothers needed during such a turbulent time; she was the lodestar in our lives.

We had our hairdressers fluff our beehives before we went out on the town, just like Jackie did. We gave dinner parties as splendid as the ones she gave (or at least we tried). And, of course, we did our best to make our children look and act like Caroline and John-John.

"Don't flap your arms at the dinner table," I'd say to Katy, who was six. "Mrs. Kennedy would never let Caroline do that!" And to Mike, age four, I'd say, "Use your salad fork, honey. You have to know which fork to use when you go to dinner at the White House."

Although we must have shouted some of these orders in anger or despair, we were sure that Jackie Kennedy's small voice, her big smile, her charm, and her very good manners would be more than enough to make her children do whatever she wanted them to do. But in our hearts, we knew they would obey her not because she was wellborn, well-off, and good-looking—a young woman who "made the best of her features" as we used to say down South—but because the heartaches of her childhood gave Jackie the strong will she needed because the ghetto of the rich can be as damaging to children as the ghetto of the poor—and it takes a strong will to get out of either one.

It was the love she had for her dashing (and wayward) father, however, that made her fall for the Senate's most dashing (and wayward) bachelor. It took a lifetime of living in fine, well-furnished houses (often in which she saw herself as an interloper) that helped her turn the rundown White House into an American showplace. There she served foods even finer than she ate as a girl, gave parties more elegant than she attended as a debutante, and charmed politicians and heads of state the way her daddy had charmed her.

It was as a mother, however, that Jackie found her true calling because nothing mattered more to her than the rearing of her children. She gave all of her spare time to Caroline and John—and some time that wasn't spare at all—and she did it, she said, for one reason: "If you bungle raising your children, I don't think whatever else you do matters very much."

It must have been hard, however, for this refined young Francophile to hold her own with Jack's big, brawling Irish family and even harder for her to instill her values in her children, especially under the influence of their wild and competitive Kennedy cousins. She prevailed, however, as she did in most things, even in the aftermath of her husband's brutal assassination, and in the direction of his state funeral. Each decision she made was classy and classically Jackie—and she was only thirty-four when she made them.

She was the one—no one else—who decided to watch LBJ take her husband's place at the swearing-in on Air Force One; to stay in her pink suit so the whole world could see her husband's blood when she got off the plane; to cover her face with a thick black veil and march from the White House—which had so clearly become her house—to St. Matthew's Cathedral for the Requiem Mass and finally to light the eternal flame on his grave at Arlington National Cemetery.

This lighting of this flame helped make Jack Kennedy's funeral one of the most memorable occasions in presidential history, but it was the salute that Jackie asked her little boy to give to his father that made it one of the saddest.

Although Jackie Kennedy had kept her children out of the public eye whenever she could, she instinctively knew that they had the right and the duty to be with their daddy on that terrible day, just as he had been with them on so many good ones.

Epilogue

WHEN I STARTED this book, I thought that my only connection to Jacqueline Kennedy Onassis would be that I happened to live in the same apartment building in New York City as she did. Yes, I had always been a fan, but Jackie's life experiences were so far removed from my own that I did not understand how she could have an influence on me. Yet, as I delved more deeply into her life, something remarkable happened. Not only did I come to appreciate what a profound impact she had on the lives of those people around her and on generations of her admirers as well as detractors but also I understood how universal the lessons from her life can be for anyone. As the work on this book progressed, I realized that her example was making a difference in my own life, sometimes in unexpected ways.

Jackie's success with men—those she knew both personally and professionally—has inspired me to experiment with a few of her techniques such as the "lighthouse look." Locking eyes with a man is not entirely new to me. Like Jackie, I found myself using it at times not necessarily connected to matters of the heart.

Jackie stayed home many nights preferring to read a good book, spend time with her children, or pursue some personal activity that gave her pleasure rather than filling the hours with outside commitments. Although I may not read the eight to ten books Jackie is said to have read every week, I find more and more that reading a good book is far more satisfying than running from party to party.

Jackie was keenly self-aware and always in touch with her feelings. She heeded her inner voice. I've ignored mine on a number of occasions, even when I knew I shouldn't, and paid the price. Jackie's life inspires me to pay attention to my intuition and act accordingly, although sometimes it is hard to do.

As a result of seeing how much Jackie accomplished in her life, I've tried to cut back on busywork and empty activities. More significant, it has made me think about what is really most important in my life. Jackie mainly spent her time doing those things that really mattered to her, not feeling guilty when she declined to do something that someone else wanted her to do. I tend to be a people-pleaser and find it difficult to say no even when I don't have the time or the inclination to do what someone asks. Jackie taught me to care as much about myself and about what I want and need as about others. She also helped me accept the fact that those I love may not necessarily want what I want but that it's okay, for me and for them.

Jackie's life had its peaks and valleys. Hers just seemed a little higher and a little deeper than others. But the courage and determination that saw her through such a remarkable life has influenced me deeply.

—Tina Santi Flaherty

ACKNOWLEDGMENTS

Writing a book is an overwhelming project, especially when you're writing about a person as beloved and talented as Jacqueline Kennedy Onassis. Those who offered encouragement and assistance made all the difference in the world.

Were it not for my publisher and editor, John Duff, the original book would never have happened. He believed in the book when it was just in the talking stage and encouraged me to go forward, and go forward once more with this commemorative edition.

This book was originally published in 2004, the tenth anniversary of Jackie's death. As the twentieth anniversary approached, John phoned me and suggested that we come out with a rerelease in 2014. His plan was to retain my original chapters, but to add new essays from notable individuals who found inspiration in Jackie's life or recognized why hers has been such an enduring legacy of courage, style, vision, and self-awareness.

At first, I groaned, anticipating all the work this would require, but I soon realized that John had a very good idea. It wasn't a slam-dunk deciding who to ask to write an essay, nor was it that easy to convince all the people I contacted to contribute. Some individuals flat-out turned me down, as they felt that their friendship with Jackie should remain private, which I can understand. I am thankful that others enthusiastically embraced the challenge and wrote beautiful and intelligent essays about a woman whose legacy deserves to live on.

I am enormously grateful to those individuals who contributed their time and talent to enhance my book with their personal reflections. These are Liz Smith, Andrew Roberts, C. D. Greene, Hank O'Neal, Ashton Hawkins, Allen Packwood, Declan Kiely, Kent Barwick, Jennifer Raab, Lynne Olson, Malachy McCourt, A. E. Hotchner, and Marguerite Kelly. I also owe a vote of thanks to my friend Edna O'Brien for allowing me to use an excerpt from her memoir, *Country Girl*.

Friends mean a great deal, most especially when one is engaged in a task like writing a book. No one could have been a better friend than Duane Garrison Pepples, who encouraged me to write this book in the first place. The keen and caring insights of Dr. Ellen Hollander were also a tremendous contribution.

The willingness of Dr. Joel Kassimir, Dr. George Lombardi, and Dr. Charles Slivinski to put me in touch with important interview prospects was also a huge help. The assistance of Emily Rafferty and Harold Holzer at the Metropolitan Museum of Art was invaluable. Ken Siman led me to a key essayist, as did Fay Rosenfeld and Lewis Frumkes of Hunter College, which made the book all the better. My friends Greg Morey and Vin Cipolla at the Municipal Art Society helped in the same regard. Dr. Ann Hohenhaus and Dr. Phil Fox at the Animal Medical Center took wonderful care of my dogs while I was writing this book and were a fount of literary inspiration to boot. Terry Decker, Iris Love, Nick Lobenthal, Peter Karadimas, Patti Printz, Martin Shea, Shirley Wu, Fritz Selby, and Mary Manges, nine very special friends, were also key supporters, which meant so much to me. My loyal staff member, Jacob Bressers, was a huge help at every step of the way. Across the pond, historians Celia and John Lee were always there for me.

Many others helped by giving information, guidance, and their time. If I inadvertently left out anyone that I should have thanked, please forgive me and know that I do appreciate your help.

I want to acknowledge my late mother, Dale Pendergrast-Santi, and father, Clement A. Santi, whose love of literature and learning illuminated my path as I wrote this book. To my sweet sister, Regina Santi Leon, I give great thanks for all her support and being there for me when I really needed her this past year, along with my kind-hearted brother, David Santi. And I give my undying gratitude to my wonderful Southern grandmother, Vattie Harvey Headrick, who not only "gloried in my spunk" but who was my cheerleader throughout her life.

Edith Wharton said that her little dog was "a heartbeat at [her] feet." I'm lucky enough to have two heartbeats at my feet—Jackie, a white Lab named after Jacqueline Kennedy Onassis, and Scarlett, a ruby Cavalier King Charles Spaniel named after the legendary Scarlett O'Hara. They both gave me much love, joy, and comfort throughout the writing of this book.

Last but not least, I will always be grateful to Winston Churchill, whose life and legacy inspire me to "never, never, never give in."

The Contributors

Kent Barwick is president emeritus of the Municipal Art Society. His past and current appointments include president of the New York Historical Society, chairman of the New York Landmarks Preservation Commission, director of the New York State Council on the Arts, and chairman of the State Council on Waterways, among many others.

C. D. Green is a celebrated fashion designer most noted for his iconic and glamorous gowns.

Ashton Hawkins is the former executive vice president and counsel to the trustees of the Metropolitan Museum of Art.

A. E. Hotchner is the author of many books, including *Papa Hemingway* and *O.J. in the Morning, G&T at Night*.

Marguerite Kelly is a syndicated columnist and coauthor of *The Mother's Almanac*

DECLAN KIELY is the Robert H. Taylor Curator of Manuscripts and head of the Department of Literary and Historical Manuscripts at the Morgan Library & Museum.

MALACHY MCCOURT is an actor, activist, columnist, and author of *Malachy McCourt's History of Ireland*, *A Monk Swimming*, and other works.

EDNA O'BRIEN is the author of *The Country Girls* trilogy and *Country Girl: A Memoir*.

LYNNE OLSON is the author of six works of history, including the bestselling *Citizens of London* and *Those Angry Days*.

HANK O'NEAL is a photographer, author, jazz aficionado, record producer, filmmaker, and concert promoter, and is the author of several books, including *Berenice Abbott: American Photographer* and his own collection, *XCIA's Street Art Project: The First Four Decades*.

ALLEN PACKWOOD is the director of the Churchill Archives Centre at the University of Cambridge, England.

JENNIFER J. RAAB is the president of Hunter College, the largest campus of the City University of New York.

DR. ANDREW ROBERTS, FRSL, is the author of *Napoleon and Wellington: The Battle of Waterloo—and the Great Commanders Who Fought It* and *Waterloo: Napoleon's Last Gamble*.

LIZ SMITH is a celebrated columnist and bestselling author of the memoir *Natural Blonde*, among other books.

The Photographs

Chapter 5: Jacqueline Kennedy Onassis at the meeting of the Committee to Save Grand Central Station. February 1977. Courtesy: AP/Wide World Photos.

Chapter 6: Jackie aboard the "Caroline," the Kennedys' private plane, reading Jack Kerouac's book, *The Dharma Bums*, 1960. Courtesy: Jacques Lowe/Woodfin Camp.

Chapter 7: Windblown Jackie walking on Madison Avenue in New York City, October 7, 1971. Courtesy: Ron Galella.

Chapter 8: Jackie with Caroline and John standing in the snow in Sun Valley, Idaho, January 1966. Courtesy: Photofest.

Notes

Jackie Revisited

"It is now all right for a woman to be a bit brainy or cultured . . . ," *New York Times,* 1/20/62.

"When asked what he was doing, he replied that he was trying to squeeze all the naughty French blood out of himself," John H. Davis, *The Bouviers: Portrait of an American Family,* 1969, p. 177.

"The prettiest little girl, very clever, very artistic and full of the devil," Mary Van Rensselaer Thayer, *Jacqueline Bouvier Kennedy,* p. 37.

"Not to be a housewife," Ibid., p. 67.

"Regal brunette who has classic features and the daintiness of Dresden porcelain," Cholly Knickerbocker, *New York Journal American,* January 7, 1948.

"She was absolutely obsessed with poverty," Sarah Bradford, *America's Queen*, p. 68.

"Like a lampshade," Jan Pottker, *Janet and Jackie*, p. 136.

"My mother had written him [Jack Bouvier] telling him she hoped he realized that he was far from welcome . . . ," Sarah Bradford, *America's Queen*, p. 72.

"We must give to life at least as much as we receive from it," Maryam Kharazmi, "Jackie is the same as Mrs. Onassis," *Kayhan International*, May 24, 1972.

CHAPTER 1: WHAT JACKIE TAUGHT US ABOUT SELF-AWARENESS

"A fan of strong drink, fast horses, and beautiful women," Barbara Walters, *20/20/ABC News*, December 17, 2000.

"If you ever have trouble with Jackie, put her on a horse," Sarah Bradford, *America's Queen*, p. 13.

"She'd seen enough downfall around her to want that insulation," Sarah Bradford, *America's Queen*, p. 68.

"We don't want any losers," quoted in Lord Longford, *Kennedy*, pp. 6–7.

"It's enough for me to enjoy a sport without having to win, place or show," C. David Heymann, *A Woman Named Jackie*, p. 116.

"It was a part of Jackie's genius . . . who to approach to help," Sarah Bradford, *America's Queen*, p. 176.

"Poor Jack, he thinks if I ignore them [the press], he'll be impeached," C. David Heymann, *A Woman Named Jackie*, p. 273.

"Maybe now people will realize that there was something under that pillbox hat." Source of quote unknown.

Notes

CHAPTER 2: WHAT JACKIE TAUGHT US ABOUT IMAGE AND STYLE

"... dose of vitamin P—praise," John H. Davis, *The Bouviers: From Waterloo to the Kennedys and Beyond*, p. 268.

"Like a mushroom," Jan Pottker, *Janet and Jackie*, p. 110.

"I was a young girl at the time . . . ," Hope Annan, interview with the author, June 6, 2003.

"Glamorous but no sex object," Letty Cottin Pogrebin, *Newsday*, May 23, 1994.

"I didn't go to Cote Basque that much," Suzanne Hemming, interview with the author, May 2003.

"Jackie Onassis was the greatest pacesetter of our time," Bill Blass, *An American Designer*, p. 72.

"I couldn't spend that much unless I wore sable underwear," Nan Robertson, "Mrs. Kennedy defends clothes; Is 'Sure' Mrs. Nixon Pays More," *New York Times*, September 15, 1960.

"In a letter . . . Jackie," Oleg Cassini, *A Thousand Days of Magic*, p. 30.

"One of the reasons President Kennedy was particularly comfortable with me was that I had been a volunteer in the U.S. Cavalry. . . ," Oleg Cassini, interview with the author, October 1, 2003.

"Even then, she always had a deft way of wearing her clothes," Robert Kaskell/Jessica Kerwin, "Fascinating Jackie," *W*, April 2001.

"We Canadians don't show our emotions," Letitia Baldrige, *A Lady First*, p. 190.

"He was proud of her. I saw it in his face," Oleg Cassini, interview with the author, October 1, 2003.

"That night Jackie abandoned her all-American wardrobe . . . ," *Time*, June 9, 1961.

"Jackie was terribly thoughtful . . . ," Oleg Cassini, *A Thousand Days of Magic*, p. 69.

"The radiant young First Lady was the Kennedy who really mattered," *Time*, June 9, 1961.

"This is Mrs. Kennedy's first semi-official trip by herself," Hamish Bowles, *Vogue*, March 2001.

"Looking like a million dollars in a suit of radioactive pink," John Kenneth Galbraith, *Ambassador's Journal: A Personal Account of the Kennedy Years*, 1969, p. 275.

"With her excellent sense of theatre," Ibid., p. 281.

"[Nehru] was greatly attracted by Jackie," Sarah Bradford, *America's Queen*, p. 218.

"My husband and I were invited to a Christmas party," confidential interview with the author, June 4, 2003.

"Before French class, we used to sit and talk on the steps of Rocky, a building named after the Rockefellers," Marlene Strauss, interview with the author, June 10, 2003.

"A mysterious authority . . . ," John H. Davis, *The Bouviers: Portrait of an American Family*, 1969, p. 345.

"Fiercely independent inner life which she shared with few people which would one day be responsible for her enormous success," Ibid., p. 345.

CHAPTER 3: WHAT JACKIE TAUGHT US ABOUT VISION

"I felt strangely let down by the White House," Carl Sferrazza Anthony, *As We Remember Her*, p. 23.

"Tattered, worn, and seemed to have no rhyme or reason," Hamish Bowles, *Jacqueline Kennedy: The White House Years*, p. 4.

"I want to make it the First House in the land," Clark Clifford, *Counsel to the President*, p. 364.

"A tale that encompasses scholarship," Maxine Cheshire, *Newsweek*, September 17, 1962.

"I had prepared a script for her which she had marked up," Perry Wolff, interview with the author, September 9, 2003.

"The Kennedys made history with their after-dinner performances in the East Room . . . ," Letitia Baldrige, *In the Kennedy Style*, p. 36.

"President Kennedy and I shared the conviction that the artist should be honored by society . . . ," Hamish Bowles, *Jacqueline Kennedy: The White House Years*, p. 8.

"It is felt by many creative figures in America . . . ," *New York Times*, November 14, 1961.

"To compare that dinner with the Casals dinner is to compare night and day," Leonard Bernstein, Oral History Program, John F. Kennedy Library.

"The chief memory I have of her is of her composure . . . her eyes wider than pools . . . ," handwritten notes and typescript of Theodore White's "Camelot interviews" with Jacqueline Bouvier Kennedy, Theodore White Papers, Box 40, John F. Kennedy Library.

"At night, before going to bed . . . ," Ibid.

"She put it so passionately . . . ," Ibid.

"I realized it was a misreading of history . . . ," C. David Heymann, *A Woman Named Jackie*, p. 419.

CHAPTER 4: WHAT JACKIE TAUGHT US ABOUT COURAGE

"She was at her best in the crunch," Martha Duffy, *Time*, May 30, 1991.

"Do you think seeing the coffin can upset me, Doctor . . . ," Donald Spoto, *Jacqueline Bouvier Kennedy Onassis: A Life*, p. 223.

"My nurse is lost," Mary Van Rensselaer Thayer, *Jacqueline Bouvier Kennedy*, p. 16.

"I was sitting beside my grandfather's coffin . . . ," Donald Spoto, *Jacqueline Bouvier Kennedy Onassis*, pp. 70–71.

"Knelt on the bench beside the coffin and put the violets down inside . . . ," Ibid., p. 71.

"Jack unloaded. . . . He confessed everything to Jackie," Edward Klein, *All Too Human*, p. 154.

"Well, my dear, I always believed in my heart that I was the one he loved," Jan Pottker, *Janet and Jackie*, p. 145.

CHAPTER 5: WHAT JACKIE TAUGHT US ABOUT FOCUS

"My press relations will be minimum information given with maximum politeness," Jacqueline Kennedy memo to Pamela Turnure. See Mary Van Rensselaer Thayer, *Jacqueline Kennedy, The White House Years*, pp. 33–34.

"Her innate control of endless details and superb sense of organization were accompanied by a quiet little phrase of iron, 'Of course it can be done,'" Letitia Baldrige, *The Kennedy Style*, p. 53.

"Darling Jimmy, I've got it . . . ," Sarah Bradford, *America's Queen*, p. 185.

"She thought I would be manageable," William Manchester, *Controversy and Other Essays in Journalism*, p. 6.

"What she saw as a courageous defense of her rights . . . ," Sarah Bradford, *America's Queen*, p. 430.

"She was an excellent student because she had 100% concentration," Tilly Weitzner, interview with the author, October 7, 2003.

"She watched the scale with the rigor of a diamond merchant," Letitia Baldrige, *A Lady First*, p. 182.

"Munching on celery and carrots," Stephen Rubin, *Memorial Tributes in the One Hundred Third Congress of the United States*, 1995.

CHAPTER 6: WHAT JACKIE TAUGHT US ABOUT THE
QUEST FOR KNOWLEDGE

"He really adored her . . . ," Sarah Bradford, *America's Queen*, p. 3.

"In those pre-television days," John H. Davis, *Jacqueline Bouvier: An Intimate Memoir*, p. 25.

"Did you understand all the words?" Mary Van Rensselaer Thayer, *Jacqueline Bouvier Kennedy*, p. 21.

"To her appreciation of the arts Jacqueline Kennedy added a passionate sense of history," Hamish Bowles, *Jacqueline Kennedy: The White House Years*, p. 3.

"Her problem at Chapin was sheer boredom," C. David Heymann, *A Woman Named Jackie*, p. 25.

". . . Miss Stringfellow says a lot of things—but I don't listen," Mary Van Rensselaer Thayer, *Jacqueline Bouvier Kennedy*, p. 20.

"You can run fast," Ibid., p. 20.

". . . the first, great moral influence," Ibid., p. 20.

"I mightn't have kept Jacqueline—except that she has the most inquiring mind we're had in thirty-five years," Ibid., p. 21.

"Jackie seldom joined in, happily staying in her room, reading, writing poetry, or drawing," Nancy Tuckerman, Sotheby's Catalogue, April 1996.

"This extraordinary girl," Stephen Birmingham, *Jacqueline Bouvier Kennedy Onassis*, p. 53.

". . . never saw her without a stack of books in hand, even when she wasn't studying," C. David Heymann, *A Woman Named Jackie*, p. 65.

"She was intellectually ahead of herself," Ibid., p. 66.

"Once you can express yourself . . . ," Caroline Kennedy, *The Best Loved Poems of Jacqueline Kennedy Onassis*, p. 168.

"I never worked harder in my life," *The World of Jacqueline Kennedy*, broadcast on NBC-TV network, November 30, 1962.

"She whizzed through the class," Sarah Bradford, *America's Queen*, p. 36.

"But when she opened her mouth and introduced herself in Italian, fluent Italian may I say . . . ," C. David Heymann, *A Woman Named Jackie*, p. 204.

"[that] she was very happy to be here in south Louisiana . . . ," Edmund Reggie interviewed by John F. Stewart, May 24, 1967, p. 50, John F. Kennedy Library, Oral History Program.

"She finished as many as eight to ten books a week," Hamish Bowles, *Jacqueline Kennedy: The White House Years*, p. 17.

"She reads as much as anybody I know—a book a day isn't unusual for her," Liz Smith, "The New York Life of Jacqueline Onassis," *Ladies' Home Journal*, February 1970.

"Read for escape, read for adventure, read for romance, but read the great writers," Caroline Kennedy, *The Best Loved Poems of Jacqueline Kennedy Onassis*, p. 168.

"It's a joy to see you work and to learn from you," confidential interview with the wife of the artist, June 22, 2003.

"I want to come back and soak it all up," Jan Pottker, *Janet and Jackie*, p. 19.

"Paris was the city that my mother loved," Caroline Kennedy, Associated Press interview, November 18, 2002.

"Whenever there was a discussion going on about the Far East . . . ," Charles Kenney, *John F. Kennedy: The Presidential Portfolio*, p. 133.

"We discussed the excavations at Samothrace," Sarah Bradford, *America's Queen*, p. 342.

"All Jackie does is read," Donald Spoto, *Jacqueline Bouvier Kennedy Onassis*, p. 279.

"What I like about being an editor . . . ," Gloria Steinem, "Why Women Work," *MS* magazine, March 1979.

"She understood what people would want to read," Betty Prashker, interview with the author, September 2003.

"I knew Jackie for many years. But it was only when we worked together that I started really to know her," Marc Riboud, *A Tribute to Jacqueline Kennedy Onassis*, 1995, p. 26.

"I was a kid in my twenties and Mrs. Onassis wanted to meet with my boss," Joannie Danielides, interview with the author, July 15, 2003.

"Given the real options of using Kennedy power or living an Onassis-style life . . . ," Gloria Steinem, "Why Woman Work," *MS* magazine, March 1979.

"... few people understood how committed and talented she was at the work she chose to do," Stephen Rubin, *A Tribute to Jacqueline Kennedy Onassis*, 1995, pp. 2–3.

"If you stop learning, you stop living in any vital and meaningful sense," Eleanor Roosevelt, *You Learn by Living*, Harper and Brothers Publishers, 1960, Foreword p. xii.

CHAPTER 7: WHAT JACKIE TAUGHT US ABOUT MEN AND MARRIAGE

"That certain something ... beauty, charm, charisma, style, any or all of the above," C. David Heymann, *A Woman Named Jackie*, p. 69.

"... when Jackie found a man ...," Ronald Kessler, *Sins of the Father*, p. 346.

"She zeroes in on you with those wide-set eyes," Ibid.

"Just give me a minute and I'll straighten this out," Richard Reeves, *President Kennedy: Profile of Power*, p. 476.

"I felt something very special in her, an understated elegance," C. David Heymann, *A Woman Named Jackie*, p. 69.

"Hey, what's wrong with that Debutante-of-the-Year cousin of yours?" John H. Davis, *Jacqueline Bouvier, An Intimate Memoir*, pp. 102–3.

"I want to live my life, not record it," Pierre Salinger, *P.S. A Memoir*, p. 209.

"The river of sludge will go on and on. It isn't about the real me," David Wise, cited in *Newsweek*, May 30, 1994.

"Go tell her to jump in the lake," Sarah Bradford, *America's Queen*, p. 6.

"... among her Bouvier cousins, she preferred the males over the females," John H. Davis, *Jacqueline Bouvier, An Intimate Memoir*, p. 30.

"Jackie had always resisted cultivating friendships with other women," C. David Heymann, *A Woman Named Jackie*, p. 206.

"He must surely have been in love with her.... He thought she was extraordinary," Cary Reich, *Financier: The Biography of Andre Meyer*, p. 261.

"He's not good enough for you, Jackie," Edward Klein, *Just Jackie: Her Private Years*, p. 194.

"Make sure Jackie's all right," Sarah Bradford, *America's Queen,* p. 416.

"She could have sold me anything from an Edsel to the Brooklyn Bridge," C. David Heymann, *A Woman Named Jackie*, p. 419.

"I'll always remember wandering Central Park on fall afternoons and all of a sudden finding her like a diamond in the grass," Ron Galella, "Jackie Onassis—Off Guard," *Good Housekeeping*, August 1974.

"All of Galella's 4,000 photographs of Jackie showed her looking exquisitely beautiful . . . ," Kitty Kelley, *Jackie Oh!*, p. 301.

Galella said, "Da Vinci had his Mona Lisa and I have my *Windblown Jackie*. The smile on the Mona Lisa is the beginning of a smile. Likewise my photo of Jackie shows her just as her smile starts. When the teeth are showing, the peak of the smile, and the moment is over," Ron Gallela, interview with the author, November 20, 2003.

"Ironically the very photographs . . . icon," Tom Ford, *The Photographs of Ron Galella*, Introduction.

"Jackie was the most interesting because No. 1, she was mobile like a deer . . . ," "Breakfast with . . . Ron Galella," Patricia Sheridan, *Post-Gazette*, June 24, 2002.

"Oh Mr. du Pont, it just shows how little we know," Donald Spoto, *Jacqueline Bouvier Kennedy Onassis: A Life*, p. 176.

"Jackie really does have a remarkably good eye. Everything looks splendid," Ibid., p. 177.

"I'd like to shake her hand first," Michael R. Beschloss, *The Crisis Years: Kennedy and Khrushchev*, p. 207.

"The tough and often belligerent Communist leader looked like a smitten schoolboy when the ice thaws along the Volga in springtime," Associated Press, June 1961.

"Oh, Mr. Chairman, don't bore me with statistics," Michael R. Beschloss, *The Crisis Years: Kennedy and Khrushchev*, p. 209.

"Within five minutes, I saw that she had the kind of magic that made you fall in love with her," Luis Rey, interview with the author, July 8, 2003.

"I just had the feeling that Jack wasn't ready to get married," Christopher Andersen, *Jack and Jackie*, p. 120.

"They had both taken circumstances that weren't the best in the world when they were younger and learned to make themselves up as they went along," Peter Collier and David Horowitz, *The Kennedys: An American Drama*, p. 191.

"All I want to do is get married to Jack," Ibid., p. 194.

"Next to my husband and my own father, I love Joe Kennedy more than anybody in the world," Christopher Andersen, *Jack and Jackie*, p. 114.

"Couldn't visualize him actually saying 'I love you' to somebody . . . ," Peter Collier and David Horowitz, *The Kennedys: An American Drama*, p. 194.

"If you're so much in love with Jack Kennedy . . . ," Jan Pottker, *Janet and Jackie*, p. 126.

"How can you live with a husband who is bound to be unfaithful but whom one loves?" Christopher Andersen, *Jack and Jackie*, p. 117.

"I loved you from the moment I saw you," Sarah Bradford, *America's Queen*, p. 258.

"An alive and vital person who had come from nowhere," Donald Spoto, *Jacqueline Bouvier Kennedy Onassis: A Life*, p. 218.

"I hate this country," Peter Evans, *Ari: The Life and Times of Aristotle Onassis*, p. 219.

"That's better than freezing there," Helen Thomas, *Dateline: White House*, p. 36.

"Cool and sharp at the edges, fiery and hot beneath the surface," Peter Evans, *Ari: The Life and Times of Aristotle Onassis*, p. 266.

"I have always lived through men," Elizabeth Peer, Lisa Whitman, and Phyllis Malamud, "Jackie on Her Own," *Newsweek*, September 29, 1975.

". . . watch the raindrops coming down the windowpane?" Gloria Steinem, "Why Women Work," *MS* magazine, March 1979.

"Jackie was my customer since I opened the store in the mid-'70s," Jimmy Ezra, interview with the author, May 19, 2003.

CHAPTER 8: WHAT JACKIE TAUGHT US ABOUT MOTHERHOOD

"If you bungle raising your children, I don't think whatever else you do well matters very much," Senator Edward M. Kennedy, *New York Times*, Eulogies, May 24, 1994.

"Until he had Caroline, he never really learned how to deal with people," Christopher Andersen, *Jack and Jackie*, p. 185.

"My mother was either at some Paris fashion house or else on her knees in some church," Edward Klein, *The Kennedy Curse*, pp. 20–21.

"I hope I do as well for my children as my mother did for me," Bill Adler, *The Uncommon Wisdom of Jacqueline Kennedy Onassis: A Portrait in Her Own Words*, p. 94.

"I believe simply in love, security, and discipline," Ibid., p. 92.

"Trust your instincts . . . you know more than you think you do," Dr. Benjamin Spock, *Dr. Spock's Baby and Child Care*, p. 1.

"I always imagined I'd raise my children completely on my own," Bill Adler, *The Uncommon Wisdom of Jacqueline Kennedy Onassis: A Portrait in Her Own Words*, p. 94.

"I think it's hard enough to bring up children anyway, and everyone knows that limelight is the worst thing for them . . . ," Carl Sferrazza Anthony, *As We Remember Her*, p. 157.

"I watched her in the White House doggedly keep a lot of time for the children," Letitia Baldrige, quoted in *McCall's* magazine, September 1994, p. 117.

"The difference between us is that you want Caroline to grow up to be like you, and I want her to grow up and be like me," Jay Mulvaney, *Diana and Jackie*, p. 165.

"I want no more—I mean this . . . ," Christopher Andersen, *Jack and Jackie*, p. 281.

"Jackie was just ferociously protective of their privacy," Ibid.

"They're entitled to some view of the White House," Christopher Andersen, *Jack and Jackie*, pp. 274–75.

"The White House would be surrounded by high brick walls," Ibid.

"She turned this drafty, cold old place into a warm environment for a young family overnight," Christopher Andersen, *Jack and Jackie*, p. 262.

"We had a dog who was named Pushinka . . . ," John Kennedy Jr., *Larry King Show*, September 28, 1995.

"The children were well-behaved because their mother would not have it any other way," Christopher Andersen, *The Day John Died*, p. 80.

"Caroline and John, usually in their pajamas and robes, were always brought in to meet the guests of honor on these occasions," Letitia Baldrige, *A Lady First*, p. 181.

"You'll see the Shah of Iran tonight, who lives far, far away in Persia," Ibid., p. 181.

"My mother helped us enormously with our creative instincts," Bill Adler, *The Uncommon Wisdom of Jacqueline Kennedy Onassis: A Portrait in Her Own Words*, p. 93.

"She really prefers to dip the brushes in water, smear the paints, and make a mess," Ibid., p. 93.

"I have found that you have to teach children concentration; it is not something they are born with," Maud Shaw, *White House Nannie: My Years with Caroline and John Kennedy, Jr.*, p. 102.

"Christina would not have recognized the little girl until she heard the mother, wearing a mask and standing in the background, say that it was time to go," anecdote attributed to Arthur Schlesinger Jr., from his book, *A Thousand Days*, p. 669.

"More time with my children . . . ," Carl Sferrazza Anthony, *As We Remember Her*, p. 157.

"Pierre, I have nothing else to do in life now except to raise my children well . . . ," Donald Spoto, *Jacqueline Bouvier Kennedy Onassis*, p. 227.

"Then will you throw me up in the air?" Christopher Andersen, *The Day John Died*, p. 124.

"Everybody knows that children are born with quite different temperaments," Benjamin Spock, *Dr. Spock's Baby and Child Care*, p. 8.

"My mother has never had an agenda for me or my sister," William Norwich, *Vogue*, June 1993.

"Please invite Caroline to everything!" Christopher Andersen, *The Day John Died*, p. 129.

"I ran into her at a dinner party in Manhattan . . . ," Fritz Selby, interview with the author, October 13, 2003.

"Caroline will have money . . . ," Murray Kempton, "The Second Act Triumph of a Tragic Queen," *Newsday*, May 22, 1994.

"Her two children turned out to be extraordinarily honest, unspoiled, and with a character equal to hers. . . . They are her two miracles," *New York Times*, May 24, 1994, p. 16.

Select Bibliography

Abbot, James A., and Elaine M. Rice. *Designing Camelot: The Kennedy White House Restoration.* New York: Van Nostrand Reinhold, 1998.

Adler, Bill, ed. *The Uncommon Wisdom of Jacqueline Kennedy Onassis: A Portrait in Her Own Words.* New York: Carol Publishing Group, 1994.

Andersen, Christopher. *Jack and Jackie.* New York: William Morrow and Company, 1996.

———. *The Day John Died.* New York: Avon Books, 2000.

Anthony, Carl Sferrazza. *As We Remember Her.* New York: Perennial, 2003.

———. *First Ladies: The Saga of the Presidents' Wives and Their Power, 1789–1961.* New York: Quill William Morrow and Company, 1990.

Baldrige, Letitia. *A Lady First.* New York: Viking, 2001.

———. *In the Kennedy Style.* New York: Doubleday, 1998.

———. *Of Diamonds and Diplomats.* Boston: Houghton Mifflin Company, 1968.

Beschloss, Michael R. *The Crisis Years: Kennedy and Khrushchev 1960–1963.* New York: Edward Burlingame Books, 1991.

Birmingham, Stephen. *Jacqueline Bouvier Kennedy Onassis.* New York: Pocket Books, 1978.

Bowles, Hamish. *Jacqueline Kennedy: The White House Years.* New York: The Metropolitan Museum of Art, 2001.

Bradford, Sarah. *America's Queen.* New York: Viking, 2000.

Bradlee, Benjamin C. *Conversations with Kennedy.* New York: W.W. Norton & Company, 1975.

Brady, Frank. *Onassis: An Extravagant Life.* New York: Ajove/HBJ Book, 1977.

Cassini, Oleg. *A Thousand Days of Magic.* New York: Rizzoli, 1995.

———. *In My Own Fashion.* New York: Pocket Books, 1987.

Clifford, Clark with Richard Holbrooke. *Counsel to the President.* New York: Random House, 1991.

Collier, Peter, and David Horowitz. *The Kennedys: An American Drama.* New York: Summit Books, 1984.

Cullinan, Bernice, and M. Jerry Weiss, eds. *Books I Read When I Was Young.* New York: Avon, 1980.

Dallek, Robert. *An Unfinished Life: John F. Kennedy.* New York: Little, Brown and Company, 2003.

Davis, John H. *Jacqueline Bouvier: An Intimate Memoir.* Canada: John Wiley & Sons, 1996.

———. *The Bouviers.* Washington, DC: National Press Books, 1993.

———. *The Bouviers: Portrait of an American Family.* New York: Farrar, Straus & Giroux, 1969.

Dwight, Eleanor. *Diana Vreeland.* New York: William Morrow, 2002.

Edkins, Diana, and Annette Tapert. *The Power of Style.* New York: Crown Publishers, 1994.

Evans, Peter. *Ari: The Life and Times of Aristotle Onassis.* New York: Charter Books, 1986.

Galella, Ron. *Jacqueline.* New York: Sheed and Ward, 1974.

Galbraith, John K. *Ambassador's Journal.* Boston: Houghton Mifflin Company, 1969.

Gallagher, Mary Barelli. *My Life with Jacqueline Kennedy.* New York: David McKay Company, 1969.

Goodwin, Doris Kearns. *The Fitzgeralds and the Kennedys: An American Saga.* New York: St. Martin's Press, 1987.

Hamblin, Dora J. "Another 'Profile in Courage.'" *U.S. News & World Report*, December 9, 1963.

Heymann, C. David. *A Woman Named Jackie.* New York: Carol Communications, 1989.

Kelley, Kitty. *Jackie Oh!* Secaucus: Lyle Stuart, 1978.

Kennedy, Caroline, comp. *The Best Loved Poems of Jacqueline Kennedy Onassis.* New York: Hyperion, 2001.

Kenney, Charles. *John F. Kennedy: The Presidential Portfolio.* New York: Public Affairs, 2000.

Keogh, Pamela Clarke. *Jackie Style.* New York: HarperCollins, 2001.

Kessler, Ronald. *The Sins of the Father: Joseph P. Kennedy and the Dynasty He Founded.* New York: Warner Books, 1996.

Klein, Edward. *All Too Human.* New York: Pocket Books, 1996.

———. *Just Jackie: Her Private Years.* New York: Ballantine Books, 1998.

———. *The Kennedy Curse.* New York: St. Martin's Press, 2003.

Leamer, Laurence. *The Kennedy Women: The Saga of an American Family.* New York: Fawcett Columbine, 1994.

Leaming, Barbara. *Mrs. Kennedy.* New York: The Free Press, 2001.

Leigh, Wendy. *The Secret Letters of Marilyn Monroe and Jacqueline Kennedy.* New York: Thomas Dunne Books, 2003.

Lincoln, Anne H. *The Kennedy White House Parties.* New York: Viking, 1967.

Longford, Lord. *Kennedy.* London: Weidenfeld and Nicolson, 1976.

Manchester, William. *Controversy and Other Essays in Journalism.* Boston: Little, Brown, 1976.

———. *The Death of a President.* London: Michael Joseph, 1967.

Marton, Kati. *Hidden Power.* New York: Pantheon Books, 2001.

Mulvaney, Jay. *Diana and Jackie: Maidens, Mothers, Myths.* New York: St. Martin's Press, 2002.

"The New York Life of Jacqueline Onassis." *Ladies' Home Journal,* February 1970.

O'Hagan, Helen, Kathleen Rowold, and Michael Vollbracht. *Bill Blass: An American Designer.* New York: Harry N. Abrams, 2002.

The Photographs of Ron Galella. Los Angeles: Greybull Press, 2003.

Pottker, Jan. *Janet and Jackie.* New York: St. Martin's Griffin, 2001.

Reeves, Richard. *President Kennedy: Profile of Power.* New York: Simon & Schuster, 1993.

Reich, Cary. *Financier: The Biography of Andre Meyer.* New York: William Morrow and Company, 1983.

Roosevelt, Eleanor. *You Learn by Living.* New York: Harper & Brothers Publishers. Reprint edition: Westminster John Knox Press, 1983.

Salinger, Pierre. *P.S. A Memoir.* New York: St. Martin's Press, 1995.

Saunders, Frank with James Southwood. *Torn Lace Curtain.* New York: Holt, Rinehart and Winston, 1982.

Schlesinger, Arthur M. *A Thousand Days: John F. Kennedy in the White House.* New York: Fawcett Premier, 1965.

Sgubin, Marta and Nancy Nicholas. *Cooking for Madam.* New York: A Lisa Drew Book/Scribner, 1998.

Shaw, Maud. *White House Nannie: My Years with Caroline and Joe Kennedy, Jr.* New York: The New American Library, 1966.

Spada, James. *John and Caroline: Their Lives in Pictures.* New York: St. Martin's Press, 2001.

Spock, Benjamin, and Stephen J. Parker. *Dr. Spock's Baby and Child Care.* New York: Pocket Books, 1998.

Spoto, Donald. *Jacqueline Bouvier Kennedy Onassis: A Life.* New York: St. Martin's Paperbacks, 2000.

Sotheby's. *The Estate of Jacqueline Kennedy Onassis: April 23–26, 1996.* New York: Sotheby's, 1996.

Thayer, Mary Van Rensselaer. *Jacqueline Bouvier Kennedy.* Garden City: Doubleday & Company, 1961.

Thomas, Helen. *Dateline: White House.* New York: Macmillan Publishing Co., 1975.

United States Printing Office. *First Lady Jacqueline Kennedy Onassis, 1929–1994 Memorial Tributes in the One Hundred Third Congress of the United States.* U.S. Government Printing Office, Washington, 1995.

Vidal, Gore. *Palimpsest: A Memoir.* New York: Penguin Books, 1996.

Vreeland, Diana. *DV.* New York: Vintage Books, 1985.

White, Theodore H. *In Search of History: A Personal Adventure.* New York: Harper & Row, 1978.

Wolff, Perry. *A Tour of the White House with Mrs. John F. Kennedy.* Garden City: Doubleday & Company, 1962.

COPYRIGHTS

Index

Page numbers in *italics* indicate photographs.

Index

funeral of
   Jacqueline Bouvier Kennedy Onassis,
     19–23, 258
   John "Jack" Fitzgerald Kennedy,
     95–96, 97, 115–17, 125, 136–37, 142,
     251–52, 261–62

Gable, Clark, 48
Galbraith, John Kenneth, 66–67
Galella, Ron, *196*, 207–11
Gallagher, Mary Barelli, 15
gardeners and battle for privacy, 243
Gates, Demi, 12
Georgetown University, 181
George Washington University, 8, 79, 176
Germany, 124
Gill, Brendan, 77
Glenn, John, 182
Glen Ora, Middleburg, Virginia, 250–51
"Glory of Russian Costume, The," 103
Goa, 64
Goldberg, Arthur, 156
good, clean fun, motherhood, 250–51
Graham, Katharine, 205
Grand Central Terminal, New York
     City, 16, 100, 103–4, 148–51, 154,
     168, 192, 194
Greece, 41, 182–83, 198
Greene, C. D., 79–81
Grill Room, Four Seasons, 52–53
"guts and gumption," 171

hairstyles, 49, 58, 62–63
half-truth vs. whole lie, crushing, 1
Hall of Mirrors, Versailles, France, 62
Hamil, Pete, 234
Hammersmith Farm, Rhode Island,
     32, 111
happiness and sadness (wedding), 14,
     110–12
Harper & Row, 139
Harriman, Averell, 156

Harrison, Edna, 176
Harris Poll, 70–71
Harvard, 202
Harvard's Radcliffe College, 257
Hawkins, Ashton, 101–4
Hemingway, Ernest, 158–59, 230–31
Hemingway, Gregory, 159
Hemingway, Hadley, 230, 231
Hemingway, Jack, 159
Hemingway, Mary, 158–59, 230
Hemingway, Patrick, 159
Hemming, Suzanne, 51
Henri Bendel, 77
Hepburn, Audrey, 50–51
Herzog, Arthur, 155
history passion, 2, 4, 6, 7, 16, 20, 21, 30, 32,
     36, 45, 50, 75, 100, 149, 167–68, 171,
     172, 175, 186, 192, 247
Honorary United States Citizenship, 123
Hoover, Herbert, 245
Horizon Press, 75
Horowitz, David, 218
horses and riding passion, 5–6, 28, 31, 47,
     51, 108–9, 119, 169, 171, 172, 251
Hotchner, A. E., 230–31
Hoving, Thomas, 102, 103
humor of Jackie, 13, 21–22, 30
Hunter College, 192
hurtful behavior, 12, 13, 27, 38, 112–14
Husted, John, 9–10, 11, 30
Huxtable, Ada Louise, 157
Hyannisport, Cape Cod, 31, 96, 257

image and style, 45–81
   celebrity status, 56, 60–61, 63, 64–65,
     118, 201
   culture influenced by Jackie, 69–71
   Diana Vreeland, 54–55, 69, 102–3
   international glamour, 61–63, 64–67
   "Jackie look," 53–55
   "official" designer, choosing an, 55–58
   parental influence, 46–50, 71

Index

O'Brien, Edna, 37–39
"official" designer, choosing an, 55–58
O.J. in the Morning, G&T at Night
  (Hotchner), 230
Old Man and the Sea, The (Hemingway),
  158
Olson, Lynne, 189–91
Onassis, Aristotle
  Andre Meyer and, 205–6
  Christina (yacht), 220
  desirability of, 30, 125–26, 197–98
  reading by Jackie and, 183
  second marriage and money, 15, 16,
    33, 118, 182, 185, 186, 197, 215,
    219–23, 229, 232, 233, 255
Onassis, Jacqueline Bouvier Kennedy,
  1–17, 105, 263–65
  arts passion, 2, 05, 6, 8, 15, 20, 28,
    35, 50, 85, 92, 93, 94, 101, 167–68,
    171, 172, 173, 175, 181, 182, 186,
    192, 248
  beauty of, 1, 5, 7, 9, 11, 20, 30, 50, 79,
    80, 97, 232
  Catholic religion of, 13, 178
  chain smoker, 70, 208
  competitive nature, 5–6, 31, 129–30
  death from cancer, 16, 104, 119–21,
    126, 193, 225
  funeral of, 19–23, 258
  grandchildren of, 22
  history passion, 2, 4, 6, 7, 16, 20, 21, 30,
    32, 36, 45, 50, 75, 100, 149, 167–68,
    171, 172, 175, 186, 192, 247
  humor of, 13, 21–22, 30
  intelligence of, 1–2, 5, 6, 7, 11, 12, 13,
    20, 34, 166, 168, 169, 170, 171, 172,
    183, 184
  literature passion, 5, 6, 13, 16, 21, 28,
    30, 34, 35, 45, 164, 165, 166–67,
    168, 171, 178–79, 183, 186, 187,
    190, 193, 264
  painting hobby, 167, 249

photographs of, *xx, 24, 44, 82, 106, 128,
    162, 196, 236*
  pilgrim soul, 234
  See also Bouvier, Jacqueline; courage;
    focus; image and style; Kennedy,
    Jacqueline Bouvier; men and
    marriage; motherhood; Onassis,
    Aristotle; quest for knowledge;
    self-awareness; vision
O'Neal, Hank, 74–78
optimism vs. pessimism, 146
Orly Airport, 61
Oswald, Lee Harvey, 115
Ottawa, Canada, 60
Our Forbears (Bouvier, J., Jr.), 4
Outward Bound course in Maine, 257

Packwood, Allen, 123–26
painting hobby of Jackie, 167, 249
Pakistan, 64, 66, 133, 180
Paley, William, 205
Palm Beach, Florida, 254
Palm Beach Post, 178
Papa Hemingway (Hotchner), 230
paparazzi, 64, 80, 207–11
Papert, Fred, 150, 151–52
parental influence on Jackie's image and
  style, 46–50, 71
Paris, France, 7, 55–56, 57, 58, 61, 92,
    130–31, 174–76, 179–80, 192, 193,
    217, 230, 231
Parish, Sister, 89
Patou, Jean, 56, 57
Peace Corps, 257
pearls, 54, 72
Pei, I. M., 16, 155–56, 157, 158
Pennsylvania, 3
People, 234
"People I wish I had known," 27
perfect choices, 60–67
Persia, 247
pet menagerie, 245–46

310

ABOUT THE AUTHOR

Paolo Giorno

A longtime admirer of Jacqueline Kennedy Onassis—and for many years a neighbor in the same New York City apartment building—**Clementina (Tina) Santi Flaherty**, author, speaker, philanthropist, and businesswoman is a former TV and radio broadcaster, who went on to become the first female corporate vice president of three of America's largest corporations: Colgate-Palmolive, Grey Advertising, and GTE (now Verizon).

Tina is the recipient of many awards and honors, including an honorary doctorate from St. John's University and American College

Dublin. She is also the recipient of an Equal People Award, sponsored by the United Nations Decade for Women. She was also selected by the National Conference of Christians and Jews as An Extraordinary Woman of Achievement.

She is an active board member for the Irish Repertory Theatre, the Animal Medical Center, the Statue of Liberty-Ellis Island Foundation Inc., and the Churchill Centre.

Tina is also the author of *The Savvy Woman's Success Bible* (with Kay Gilman) and *Talk Your Way to the Top.* She lives in New York City with her two dogs, Jackie and Scarlett.

Visit her on Facebook and follow on Twitter @TinaSFlaherty.